STANDARD

STANDARD ARCHITECTURE | DESIGN

Artifice

CONTENTS

ANOTHER INTERPRETATION (IN NINE PARTS)

Mimi Zeiger

"No, I don't think that it's geniuses we need now. I think geniuses are events, not goals or ends. Neither do I believe that we need pontification about architecture, or grand doctrine, or prophecy, always a dubious affair. We still have something with a living tradition within our reach, as well as plenty of moral tenets concerning ourselves and our craft or profession as architects (and I use these terms in their best traditional sense). It is necessary for us to make good use of the little that still remains of a tradition of construction and, above all, morality in an age in which the most beautiful words have lost virtually all their real, true, significance."
—José Antonio Coderch, *Domus*, 1961

Enter Backwards

Standard's office is located at the easternmost side of Santa Monica Boulevard in a blank-eyed building on a nondescript block. Far west, the boulevard ends at the seaside. There, the pier is flocked with tourists, and the Ferris Wheel spins continuously. But at the east end, just a few hundred yards before unceremoniously merging with Sunset Boulevard, there's no spectacle: a famous gay bar on one corner, a greasy taco stand on the other. With little coyness, Standard is hiding in plain sight—a method they employ often in their work. The facade offers few hints. Is it a house, a storefront, a converted garage? The banal ambiguity of the setting is fitting for a firm that deftly shuns the expectations of contemporary architectural practice or, at least, the hubbub of media and the stylized dynamics of starchitecture and today's high-flying design culture. Partners Silvia Kuhle and Jeff Allsbrook aren't interested in all that, despite several high-profile retail and art world clients. Instead, their headquarters suggests Ed Ruscha's deadpan photographs and the black-and-white stillness of his Sunset Boulevard facades.

To reach Standard's office you must enter backwards. A small sign tacked to a neatly painted door informs visitors to continue down the driveway. Keep walking until you find yourself at a sun-bleached backyard. The materials of the street are uncannily transformed: sidewalk cement becomes smooth concrete and pea gravel replaces blacktop asphalt. An oversized sliding glass door nearly fills the rear facade—pushed open, it's a warm yawn of an invitation. This is the entrance.

It's tempting to simply assign these routes from curb to threshold a vintage architectural term like sequence or procession, yet to do so reduces the experience to mere trope. What's at play here is a kind of spatial reflexivity. Premeditatedly elliptic, Standard contradicts the era's impulse for reinvention and disruption and the subsequent requirement that new architectural expressions reflect the march of progress through brand or signature.

Systems and Their Effects

As with their studio, one must enter Kuhle and Allsbrook's house backwards. A construction of glass, wood and concrete, their home, the Tree House, is hidden behind a mid-60s carriage house in the Silver Lake hills. To reach it, a visitor must navigate a steep set of steps that are tucked along the flank of the older building, while the new structure looms above. The payoff for the hike is a 180-degree view.

One late afternoon Kuhle sits in an Eames Aluminum Group lounge chair in her living room, silhouetted against a hazy blue Los Angeles sky. Design culture has elevated the chair's older sibling, the beefy plywood lounger, to a mid-century icon. This streamlined chair, less so. Functional, not cushy. Corner office, not man cave.

Her shins graze the ottoman. "I don't view buildings as objects," she declares.

Lest the line seem unbearably dogmatic, let's add context. We're discussing her architectural training at the Technische Universität in Darmstadt, Germany, where she studied before embarking on graduate work at Columbia University. Rooted in Modernist pedagogy, the school instilled a functionalist approach to architecture, even while other institutions in the late 1980s followed more theoretical trends. Her student work was infrastructural: a train station in post-wall Berlin or "traveling beach" off the coast of Germany and Holland that would create an artificial shoreline as it moved.

"It was all systems and effects," she adds.

The statement is telling. The building as a mechanism—a kit of parts of systems, materials and program—is a counter-narrative in twentieth-century architectural history. From Mies van der Rohe to Rem Koolhaas, architects have argued for non-objects. Standard doesn't design buildings to stand out as objects. But neither do they avoid form, to say so would ascribe default informality to their very precise work. Instead, the architects value formal rigor over gestural experimentation. A project such as the Mission Road gallery for New York's Michele Maccarone, for example, strips down the former 1920s clothing factory (an artifact of industrialization of the kind that influenced early Modernism) to essentials. Existing wood beams and skylights establish a rhythm of structure and natural light within the all-white 12,000-square-foot gallery. The only real proof of architectural intervention is a single freestanding wall bisecting the gallery. The rest is all systems and effects.

A Tile Roof on a Miesian Box

To be an architect In Los Angeles, especially if you design residences, is to continually reckon with the ghosts of California Modernism. Mid-century masters haunt this town: Rudolph Schindler, Richard Neutra, Gregory Ain and others. To ignore them or even outright reject them is a statement of negation and an erasure of history. To embrace them risks nostalgic imitation and parroting of the relaxed tenants of the period such as a flow between inside and outside or post and beam construction. A contemporary practice, then, needs to set its own rules of engagement.

"I consider myself a Modernist, I definitely put myself in that category, but I wouldn't want to be seen as someone who's paying homage to those guys," Jeff Allsbrook explains as part of a long, wide-ranging conversation about Standard's work. The architects aim to create a new take on Modernism that isn't explicitly pegged to mid-century design. We are seated in the living room of the home the architects designed for themselves, and he looks up to the ceiling—it's a structural cantilever that extends past the window wall to create a balcony above—and tells me that they were conscious not to express the beams.

"Still, we do look at history," says Kuhle.
"But we don't practice historical styles," adds Allsbrook.

Instead, the pair looks beyond the West Coast to places where other expressions of Modernism took shape like Europe and Latin America. Several days later at Standard's office, Allsbrook pulls a book off the shelf, an old volume on the Spanish architect José Antonio Coderch that's part of the architects' library of somewhat anachronistic reference material. (He was first introduced to Coderch's designs while working and studying abroad in the late 1980s and early 90s.) He flips open the cloth cover to show me the houses, black and white photographs of low-slung single-family homes set in a Mediterranean landscape. Absolutely a Modernist, Coderch was part of CIAM, but he didn't ascribe to any stylistic doctrine. Like Standard, or Standard like him, he played by his own rules. Allsbrook describes the Ballvé House in Camporón as "a Miesian floor plan with a Spanish tile roof". And it is. Built in 1957, the floor plan, with its long brick walls, references Mies' Brick Country House from 1923, but topped with an almost vernacular roof. "There's a very clean minimal edge to the roof that distinguishes it from a traditional house," Allsbrook explains, seemingly relishing both the perversity of juxtaposition and the elegance of how the detail was resolved. For Standard, history offers design solutions, not dogma.

1973 Karmann Ghia

In the mid-1990s, when Allsbrook and Kuhle moved to Los Angeles (years before Standard became the firm it is today) the city was still reeling from the impact of the 1992 LA Riots. Los Angeles, always a place of multiple centers and diverse neighborhoods, had fragmented into enclaves. Compared to the urbanism they had lived overseas—dense, walkable cities rich with cafes, history, art and architecture—the place seemed foreign. The pair drove around town in a 1973 Karmann Ghia, a European car made for navigating the Autobahn, not the 405 Freeway. The strangeness of the sprawl only heightened the feeling that Los Angeles was living up to its stereotype.

Eventually, the city revealed itself, offering up a seductive domestic urbanity. Private spaces—friends' living rooms or back yard patios—became places of thinking, critical engagement and conversation. The seeming wildness offered opportunities too. With the distinctions between high and low culture blurred, the old hierarchies of society and connections as a way of finding clients dropped away. "I think a lot of people in Los Angeles that are successful, are self-made and therefore, when they see you and you're younger, they're willing to take a chance on you," says Kuhle, recalling Standard's first real break, a commission from Tommy Perse, father of James Perse who would later ask Standard to not only design his home but also apply their sensibility to his retail brand and its spaces.

Today, Los Angeles has matured—its sunburnt noir tidied up with new development and infrastructure. "Los Angeles has evolved since 1994," says Allsbrook. "The art galleries, the museums, the fashion stores, all of it has changed over those years." These transformations track with Standard's growth and offered new opportunities for architecture. The firm's projects include retail storefronts for local and international fashion labels and spaces for the art world clients moving into Boyle Heights and South La Brea—spots in the urban fabric that would have seemed too edgy two decades ago.

Inside Out

There's a small black-and-white drawing that's pinned to the wall of Standard's office: a site plan of Melrose Avenue as it terminates into North Doheny Drive in West Hollywood. Shaded in gray are the locations of four stores all within a block from each other and all designed by Standard: Jenni Kayne Apparel + Home, James Perse, Maxfield Gallery and Helmut Lang. Easy to miss amongst the color photographs, the printout tells a story about the firm's approach to retail design. Each of the projects is conceived as both themselves—retail destinations—and also part of the greater urban fabric. As such, the projects respond to the scale of the neighborhood, where most of the buildings are one- and two-story structures, and to the pedestrian character of the street. The storefronts don't broadcast the brand with the brashness of a billboard, but rather entice at a domestic scale.

"For us, to design a store for a brand is to design its cladding," explains Allsbrook. "The cladding becomes the sign for the store, or at least it communicates the brand's message. They're not places of spectacle; for the most part they communicate that this could be a place you want to live in." This is certainly true of the Jenni Kayne flagship store on Almont Drive, just off Melrose. Although the building began life as a warehouse, Standard's transformation of the space operates in a residential vein. The entrance is positioned not front and center, but on the side of the building. Shoppers then pass through a series of thresholds: iron gates, vestibule and wood-clad doors. The procession is closer to arriving at a home than a store. If there's a quietude to their storefronts, then inside the architects devote their energy to using ordinary materials—concrete floors, exposed beams, wood siding—to create spatial and aesthetic effects.

If in the old architectural adage, ducks equal heroic gestures, and decorated sheds are signage or ornament tacked onto a utilitarian structure, Standard flips the script. In a continuation of how the firm works with reflexivity (and in this case, inversion), Allsbrook describes their retail projects as "inside-out decorated sheds, not ducks".

Hiding in Plain Sight

Kayne Griffin Corcoran Gallery is located deep in Los Angeles' Mid-Wilshire neighborhood on a block of South La Brea Avenue that is home to auto body repair shops, a questionable motel and a McDonald's. It's the kind of landscape that is indicative of a changing city: new art spaces shoulder to shoulder with the mix of ugly and banal twentieth-century commercial architecture. Their years in Los Angeles have given Standard an appreciation of the sprawl and as mainstream culture reclaims the urban realm, dissipating old myths that cities are scary or unlivable, the firm has developed certain stealth tactics for design, namely the fence and the courtyard.

With Kayne Griffin Corcoran Gallery, the firm maintained the 15-foot-tall perimeter walls of the existing warehouse. Overgrown with vines, the building hides in plain sight. Ordinary, it's masked from view. A refined black steel gate is the one hint that something other than a mechanic's yard lies beyond the fence. Standard used industrial steel paneling (a vernacular material), but honed the details of the custom gate. Visitors must be buzzed into the gallery, a security gesture, but once beyond the threshold, they are welcomed into a different world: lush courtyard and sculpture garden edged by light-filled galleries. Similarly, a long steel fence and gate act as a stealth facade for Standard's Maccarone Gallery on Mission Road in Boyle Heights. Made out of three layers of expanded metal, the gate retains some porosity between the street and the large sculpture courtyard beyond.

While gates and fences might suggest a defensive approach to a neighborhood—a regression to the fears of earlier decades—their use can also be read as a counter position to the ingratiating pop-up urbanism that has marked development in Los Angeles and beyond. Standard's is a reticent urbanism that embraces the ordinary as status quo. Privacy trumps publicity as their approach continues a history of outdoor spaces drawn from domestic architecture, such as backyard patios and courtyard apartment buildings.

Redefining Luxury

Over email Allsbrook tells me that Alison and Peter Smithson's 1974 essay "Without Rhetoric-An Architectural Aesthetic 1955-72", which he read as a graduate student living Europe, made a significant impact on his early work. In it, the Smithsons lay bare their influences (advertising, American engineering and manufacturing, the city of Bath, among others) in order to argue a retroactive manifesto for their work to date. Of their hero they write, "Mies had a special feeling for materials as luxury.... [T]he luxury rests in the fact that the observer is made aware of the essence of each material."

Standard's work is similarly reductive, finding luxury in simple finishes: a polished concrete floor or precision stone and marble surfaces. "If you want to summarize what we have to do for our clients, it's create spaces of desire," Allsbrook explains, as we sit in the living room looking out on a luxurious view of Los Angeles. The architects are interested in how you experience spaces and materials, and how a client or visitor might relate to the architecture. This is true as much for the retail clients as for homes and galleries.

Luxury, then, is not about expense or flash, but about coaxing a feeling of desire from even the most basic materials. The architects work through iteration after iteration to hone a design and material palette, and there's a luxury in being able to apply the time and expertise needed to mind a minimal solution. While Modernism provides lessons for how they navigate a particular project, the firm is chasing a larger project, one with an embodied tension: they aim for timeless design in a city of rapid change.

"We write to make ourselves see what we have got in the inescapable present... to give another interpretation of the same ruins... to show a glimpse of another aesthetic."

—Alison and Peter Smithson, "Without Rhetoric", 1974

RESIDENTIAL

TREE HOUSE

Los Angeles, 2004

Perched near the top of a hillside in Los Angeles, and enveloped by a large ash tree, the house responds to its site and the city through its transparent southern exposure. Accessed via a long stair through the landscape, the house offers panoramic views of the Los Angeles basin upon arrival to its entry.

A partially concealed post and beam structure modulates the exterior and allows openings to span from floor to ceiling. The second floor bears on thin stainless steel columns and cantilevers over a concrete deck, which in turn cantilevers over the slope of the hillside. The horizontal layering of the roof and floors extends the interior and engages the space beneath the ash tree. The strong horizontal projections provide visual balance to the tree's immense trunk and limbs. Redwood siding clads the overhangs and defines the transition between the inside and outside.

The house enjoys a microclimate that significantly reduces reliance on mechanical systems, by employing passive solar design, convective air movement and the large tree as climate control. The tree's shade and transpiration cool the house during the hot summer months, and it lets the sun in after the leaves drop during the late fall and winter. During most of the year the large sliding door on the main level is open, uniting the terrace and the living areas as one space under the tree.

Site plan

South facade

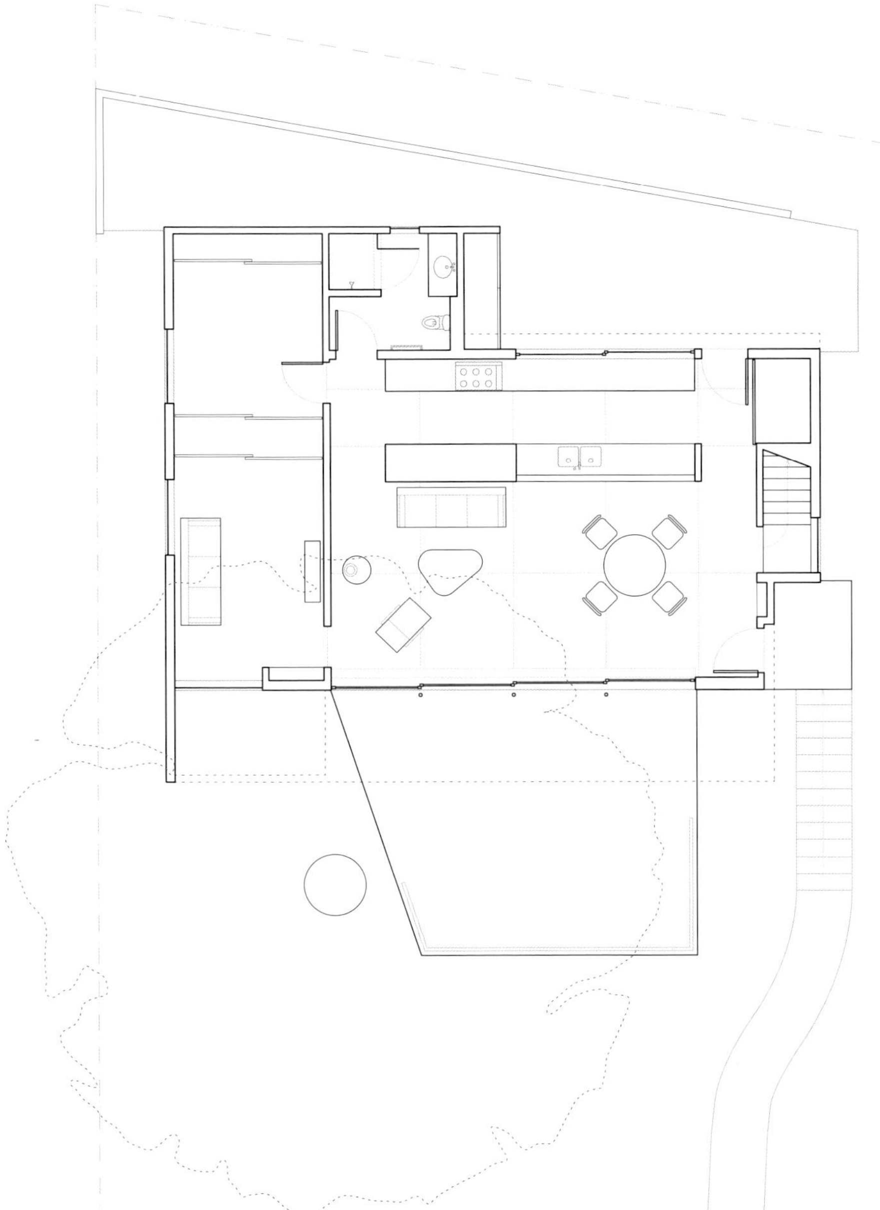

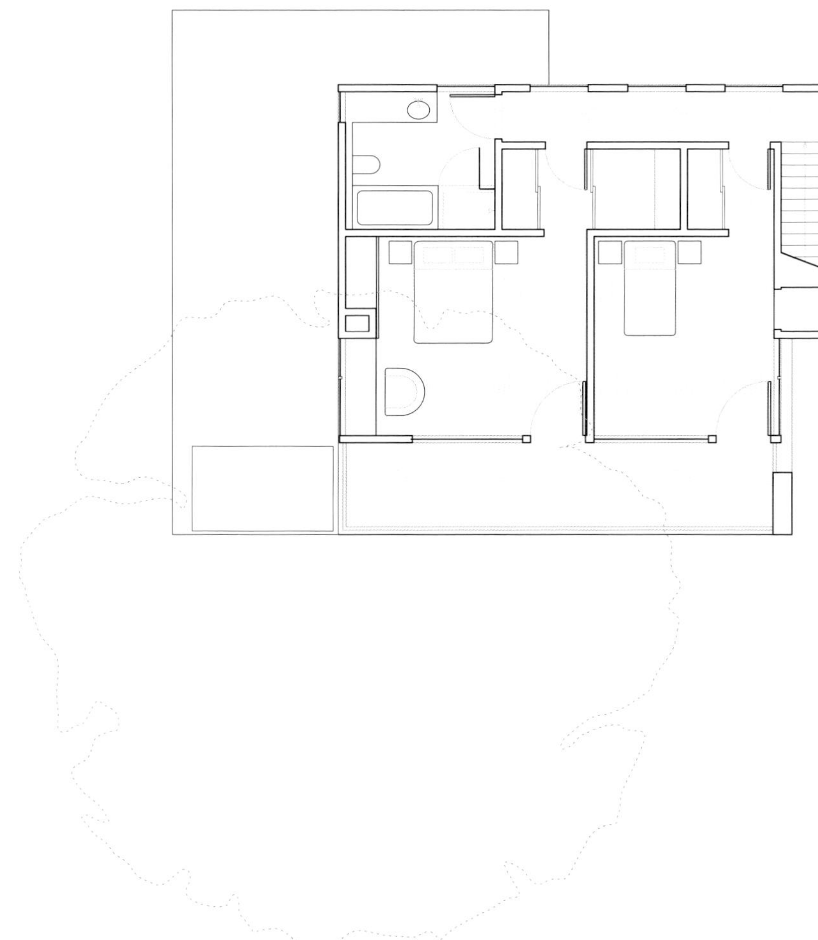

Ground floor plan Upper floor plan

Living room Bedroom South facade

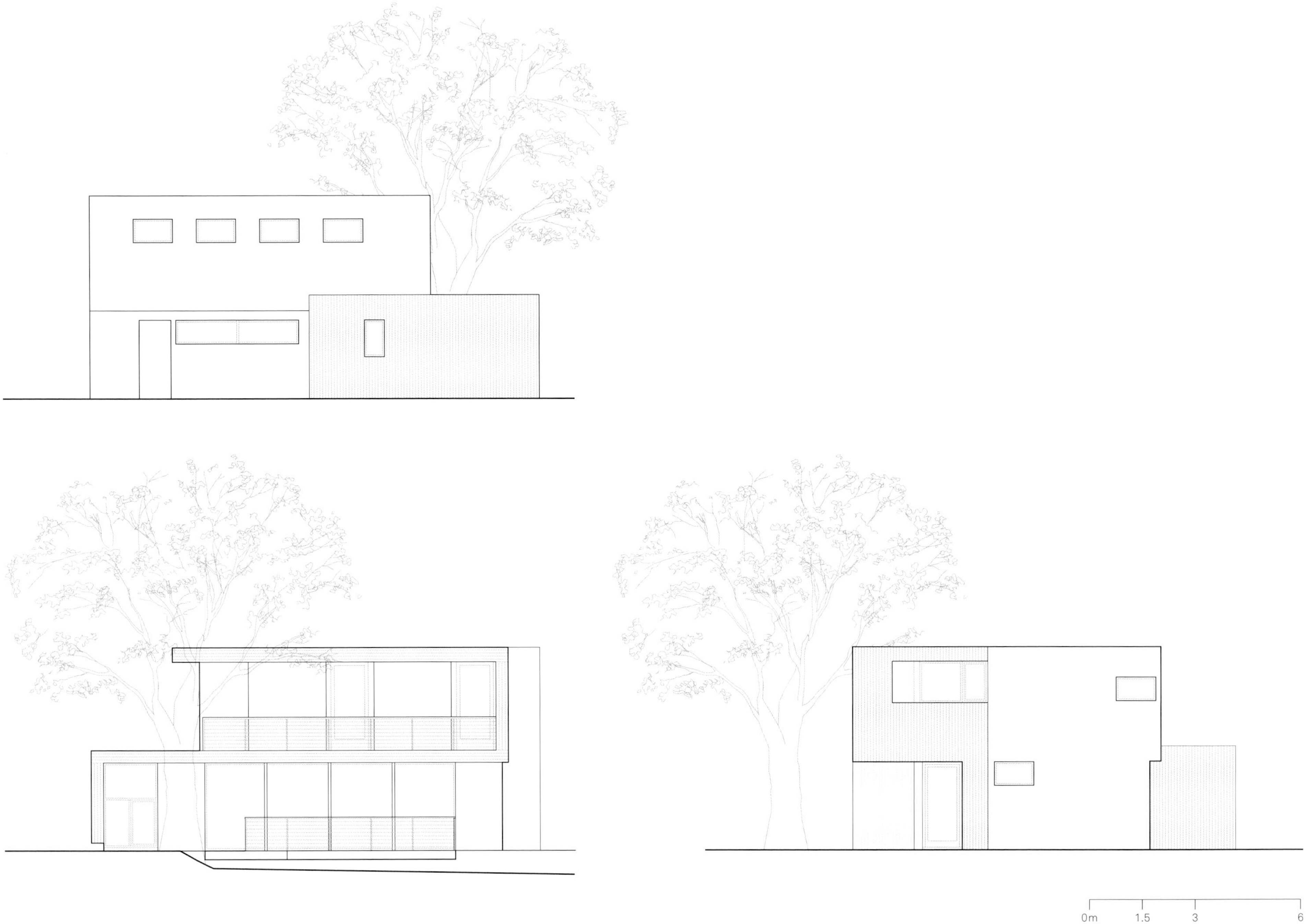

North elevation South elevation East elevation

South facade

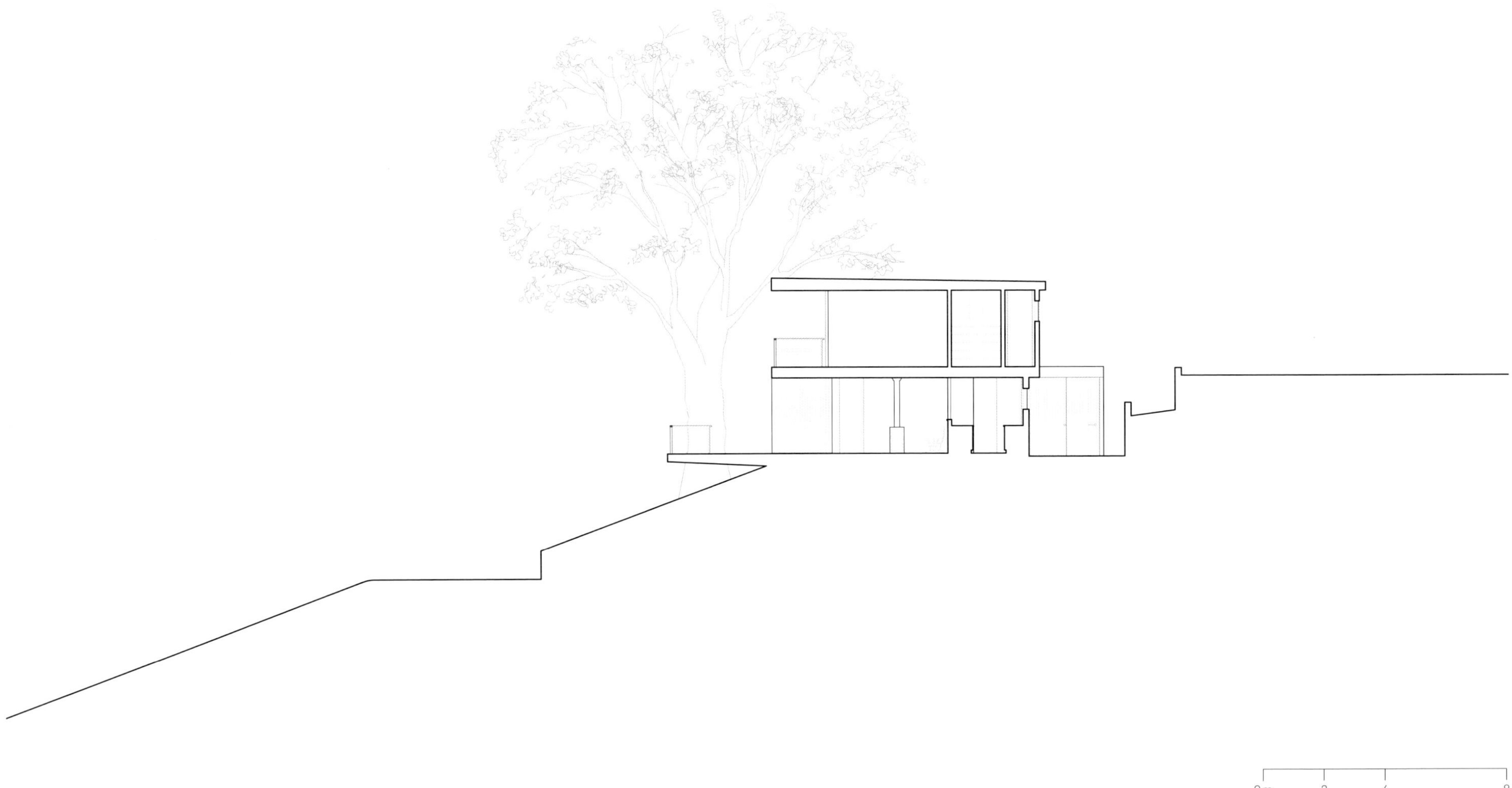

Cross section

Detail of south facade

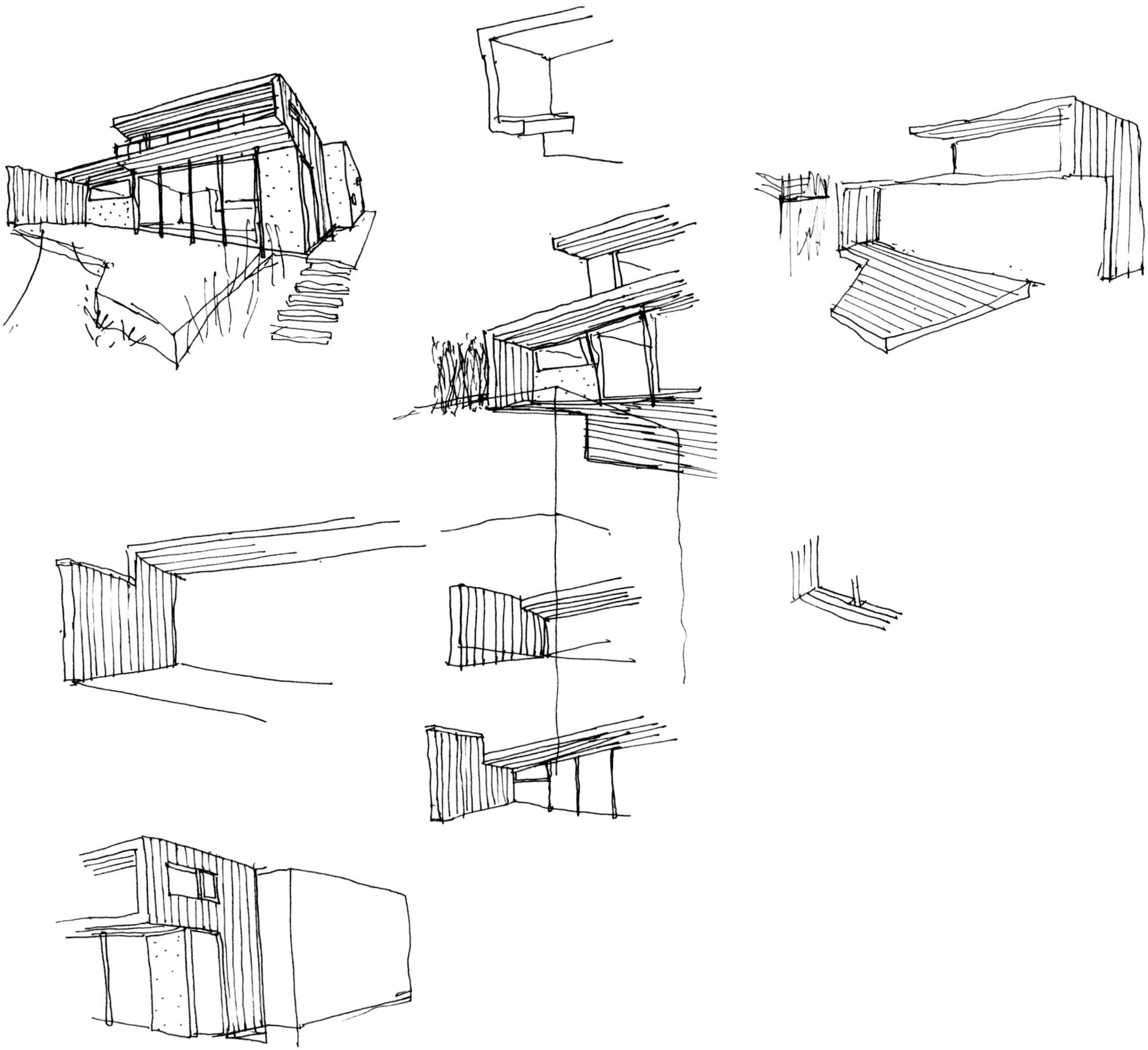

Kitchen

South facade

HIDDEN HOUSE

Los Angeles, 2007

The serene Hidden House offers limited views of downtown Los Angeles, yet seems like a world away from the city. The house was rebuilt and expanded on the foundations of a former 1940s cottage. Vestiges of the former house remain as individual rooms attached to a larger L-shaped open plan, which forms two large outdoor rooms oriented toward the city and the canyon, respectively.

The new and the old are integrated though a consistent approach to exterior materials. The east–west walls are covered with cement plaster, while the north- and south-facing walls are clad in wood siding. The house is constructed from sustainable materials ranging from Californian redwood cladding to reclaimed end-grain wood flooring and cork flooring.

Outside, wood decks lead to concrete patios that are scaled like interior rooms. Six large wood and glass pivot doors link the two courtyards through the living/dining room. From the informal areas of the house, a 24 foot wide sliding door pockets into the wall, creating a seamless indoor–outdoor connection.

Daily life centers around the canyon courtyard, which transitions to an expansive yard that is given over to kitchen gardens, an organic flower farm and a chicken coop. Other areas are landscaped with native flora such as Oaks, Sycamores and Manzanita. The house, equipped with solar panels, is designed for cross ventilation and natural lighting. The maturation of the landscape trees will further reduce cooling loads through shading.

Site plan

Aerial view

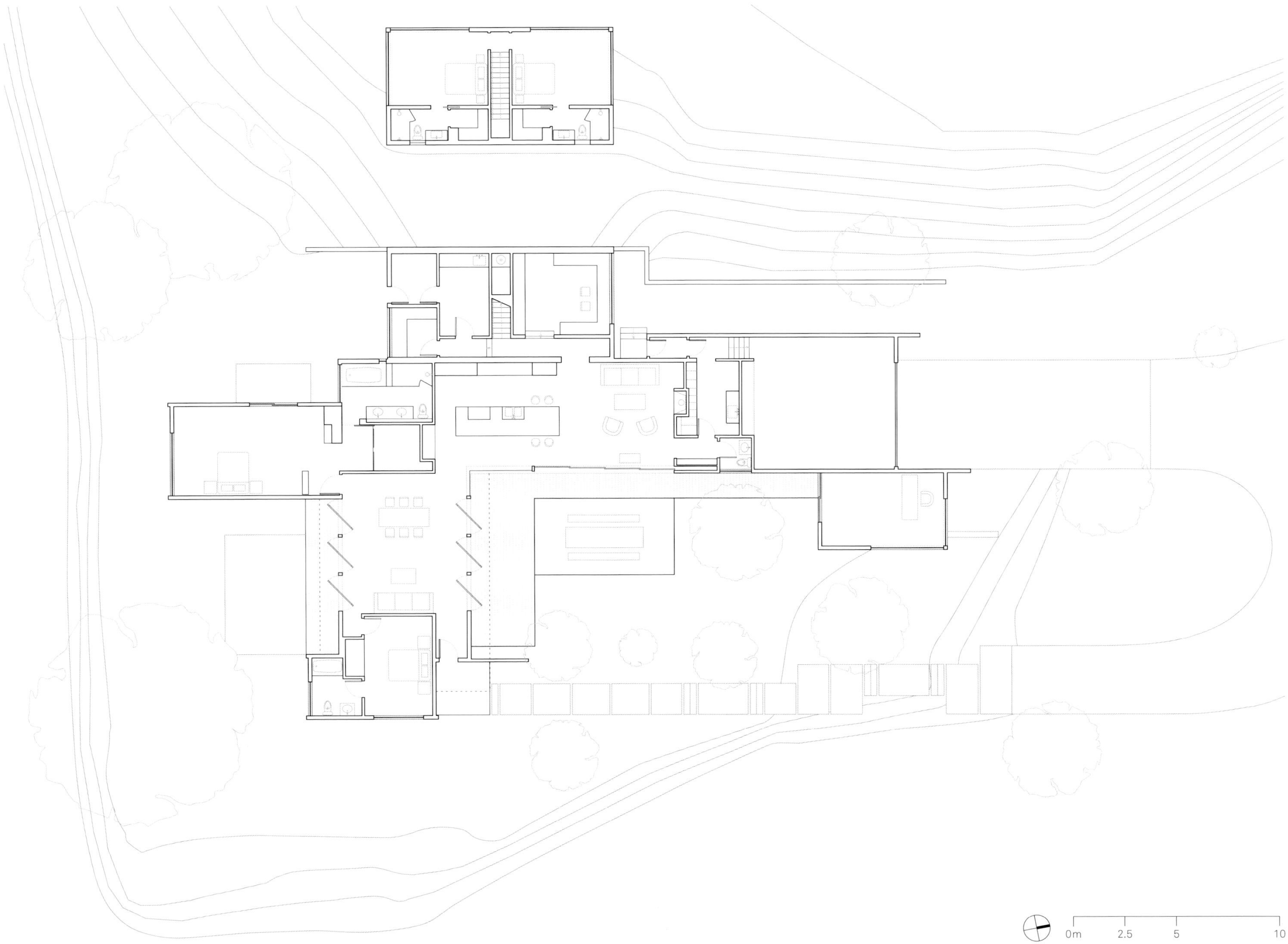

Upper floor plan Ground floor plan

South-facing patio

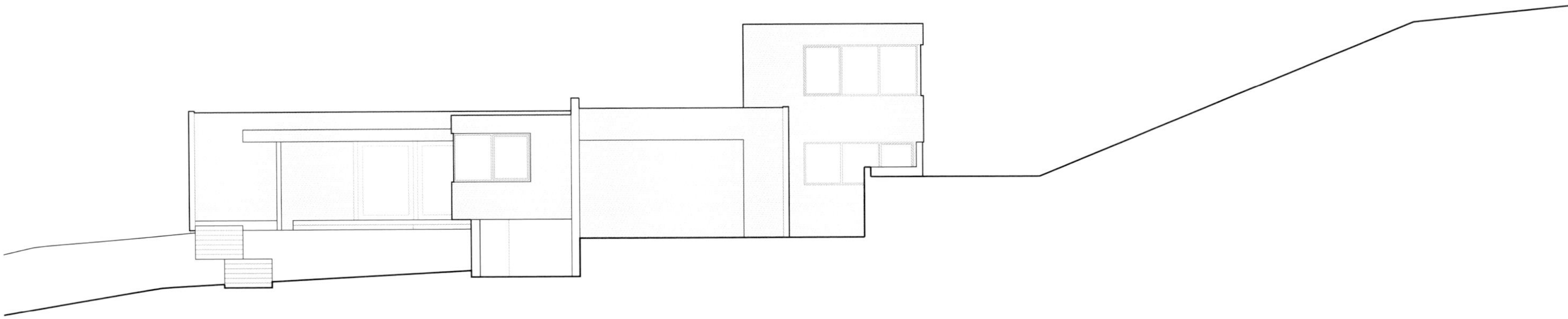

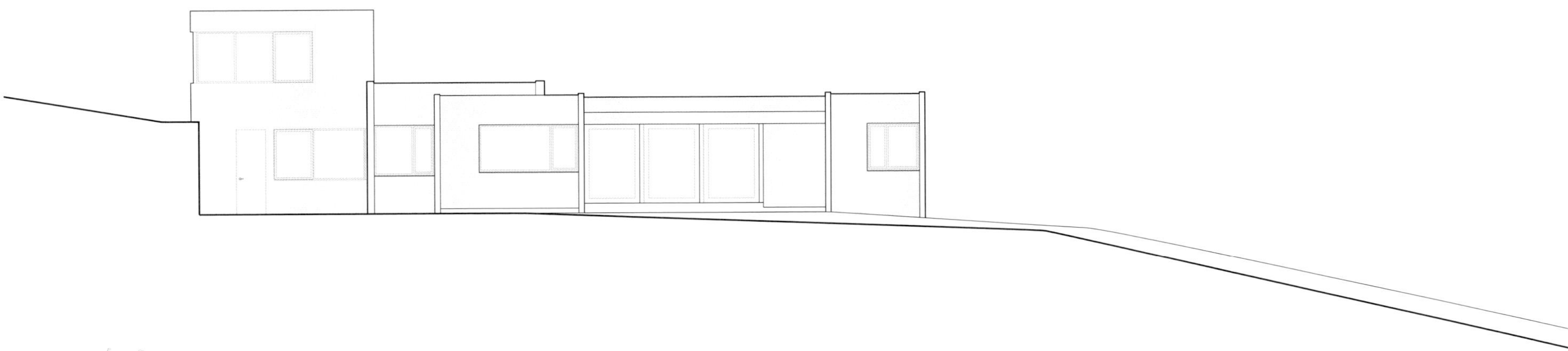

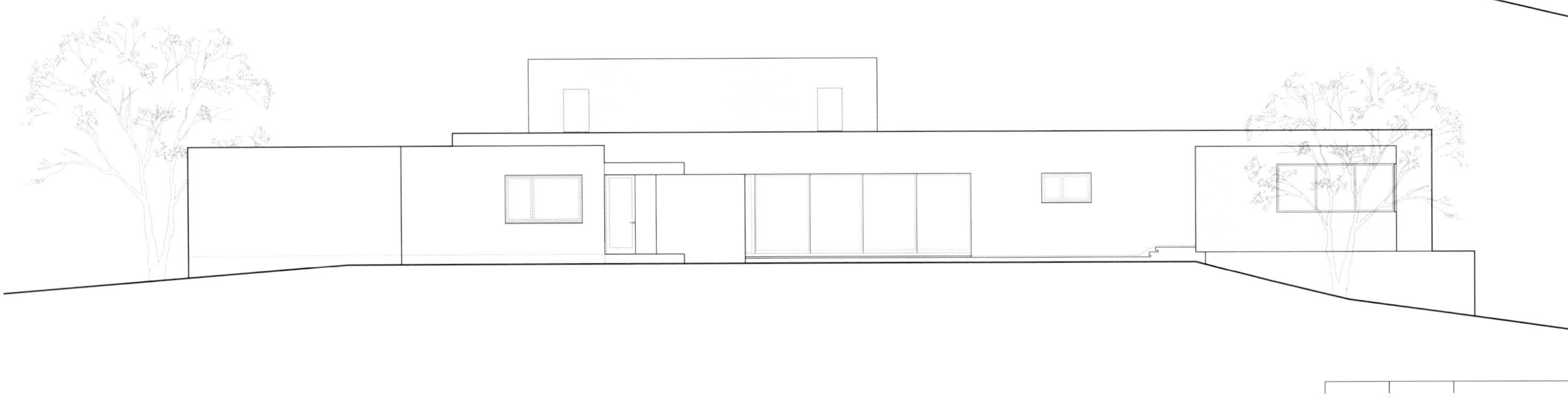

North elevation

South elevation

East elevation

Kitchen and family room

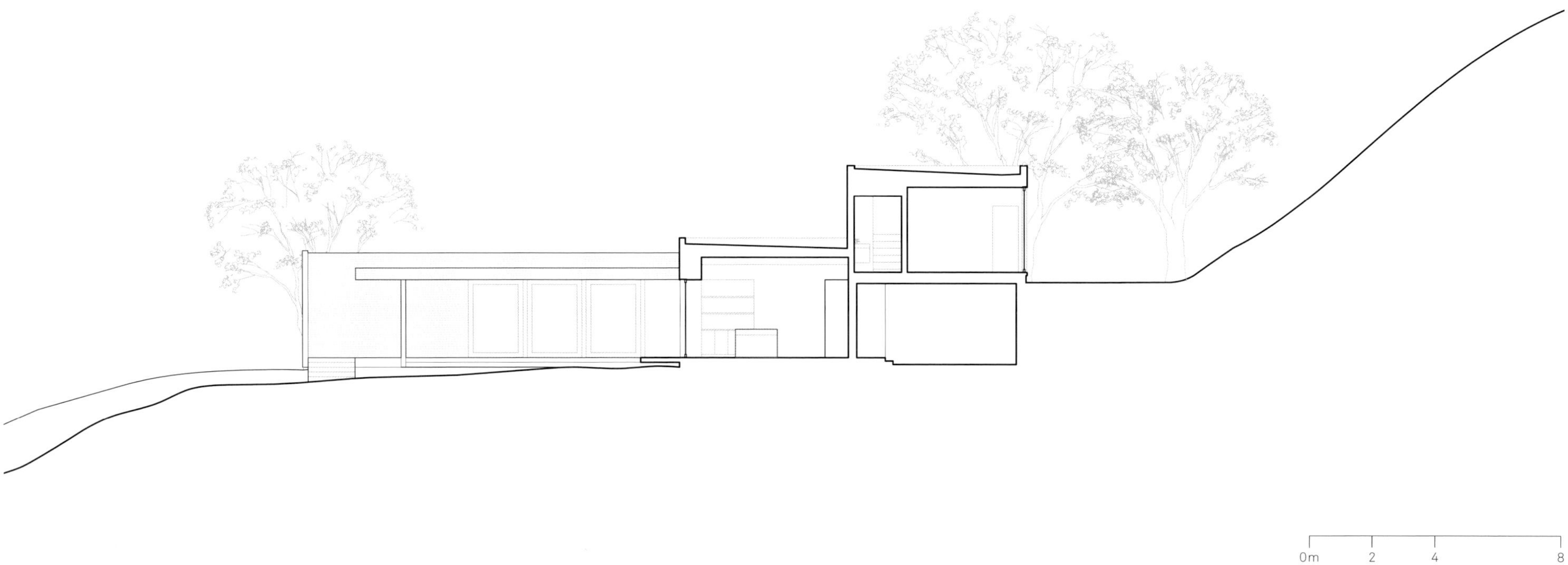

Section

Glass corner

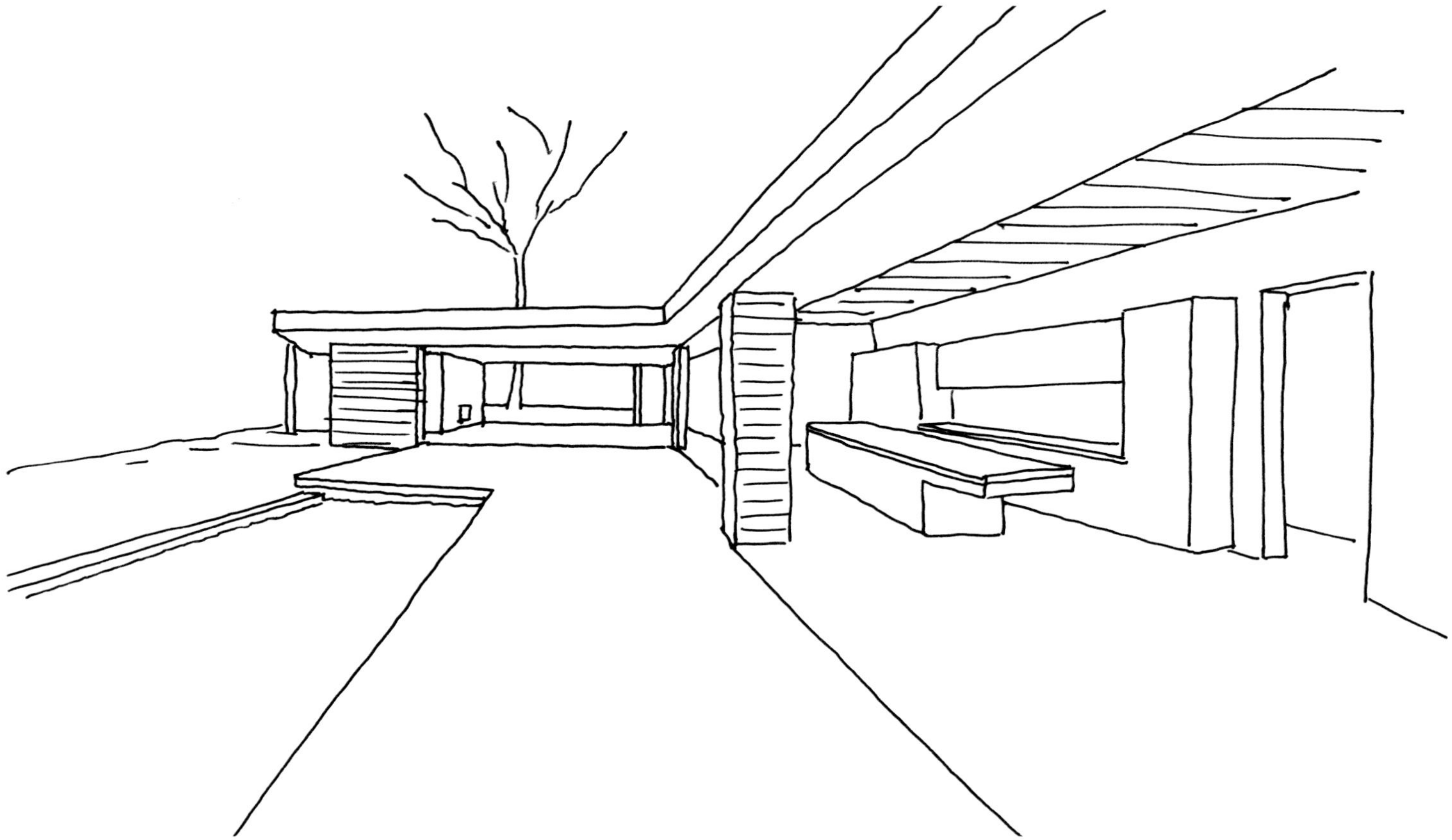

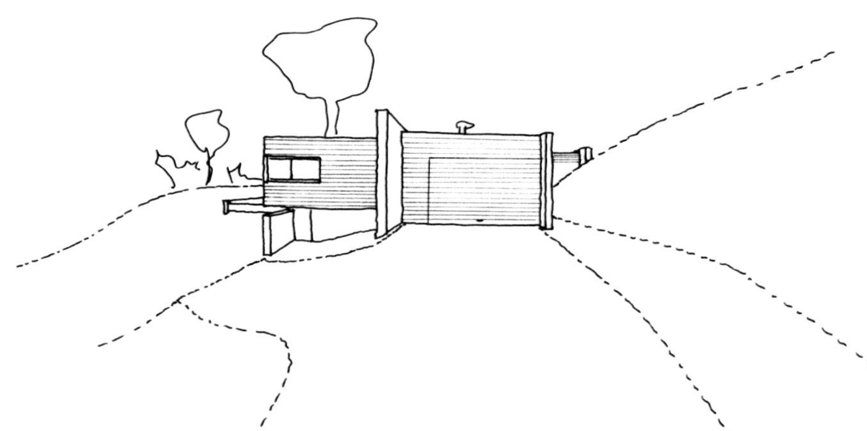

Perspective studies

Dining room Entry path East-facing courtyard

MODERN SPANISH HOUSE

Los Angeles, 2016

Standard was commissioned to re-imagine the Taylor/Lippiate residence, originally designed by architect Roland Coate in the late 1920s. Designed in the Spanish Colonial style, the award-winning original design was altered over the years to conceal much of its Spanish influence, especially on the interior. The design approach for the project respected Mr. Coate's work where it was still extant, and otherwise interpreted Spanish style on contemporary terms.

The house is situated between a cul-de-sac and a golf course landscape, but was closed off from its setting. By creating large new openings in the walls and installing rows of pivot doors, the interior of the house was lightened and opened to the green expanse of the golf course. The rear landscape, overlooking the links, was regraded and terraced to visually extend the interior floor level to the outside.

Inside the house, the floor plan was altered to create a modern open kitchen, and to accommodate the client's program. The existing entry and grand living rooms were excavated to remove years of decoration. An original coffered ceiling was found and restored in the bar area, and original riveted steel beams were left exposed in the living room. The rest of the interior was completely redesigned and reclad to give the home a lightness and openness that it lacked. Taking a cue from the coffered bar ceiling, the entry, dining and family room ceilings were designed with beams to conceal the lighting. A 17-foot-tall arched oak door was designed for the two-story foyer, and white arched openings were introduced as transitions between the main rooms. Danby marble covers the long entry stair, the grand entry floor, and extends flush to the patios at the rear of the house. The house retains its original massing and character from the exterior, which belies the new airy interior.

Site plan

Entrance steps

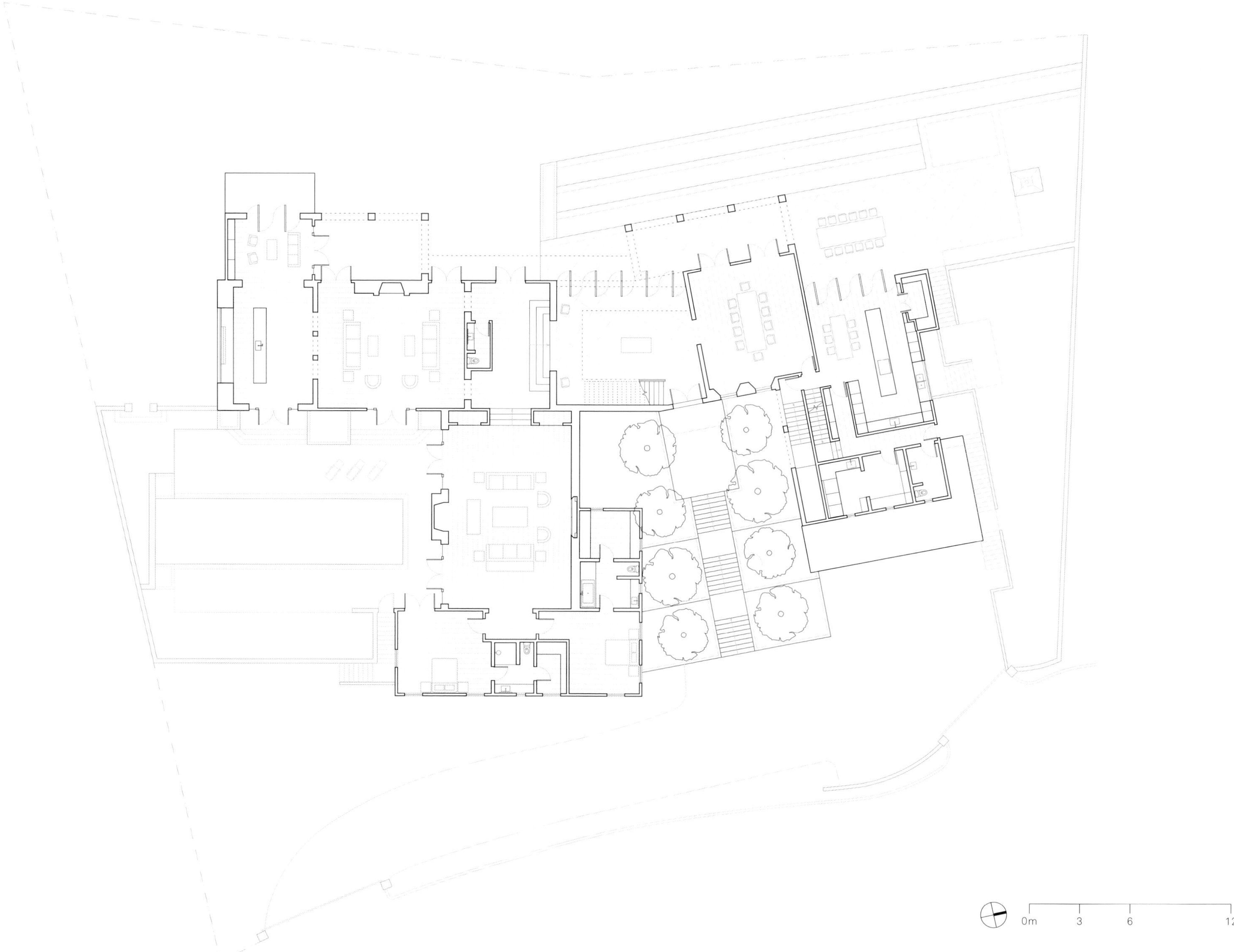

Ground floor plan

Entrance

Foyer

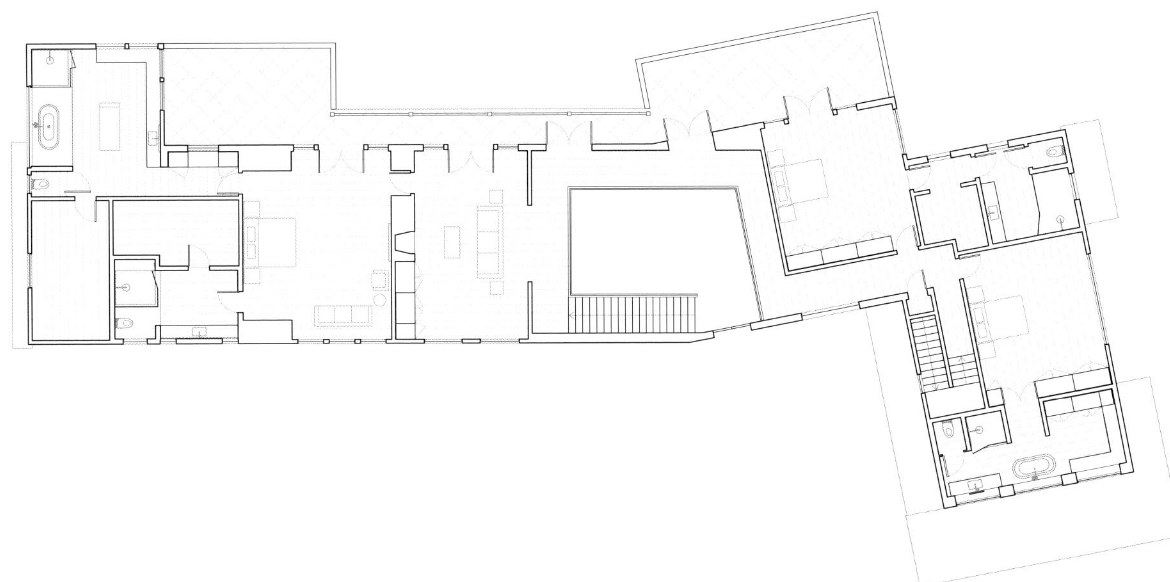

Upper floor plan

Living room

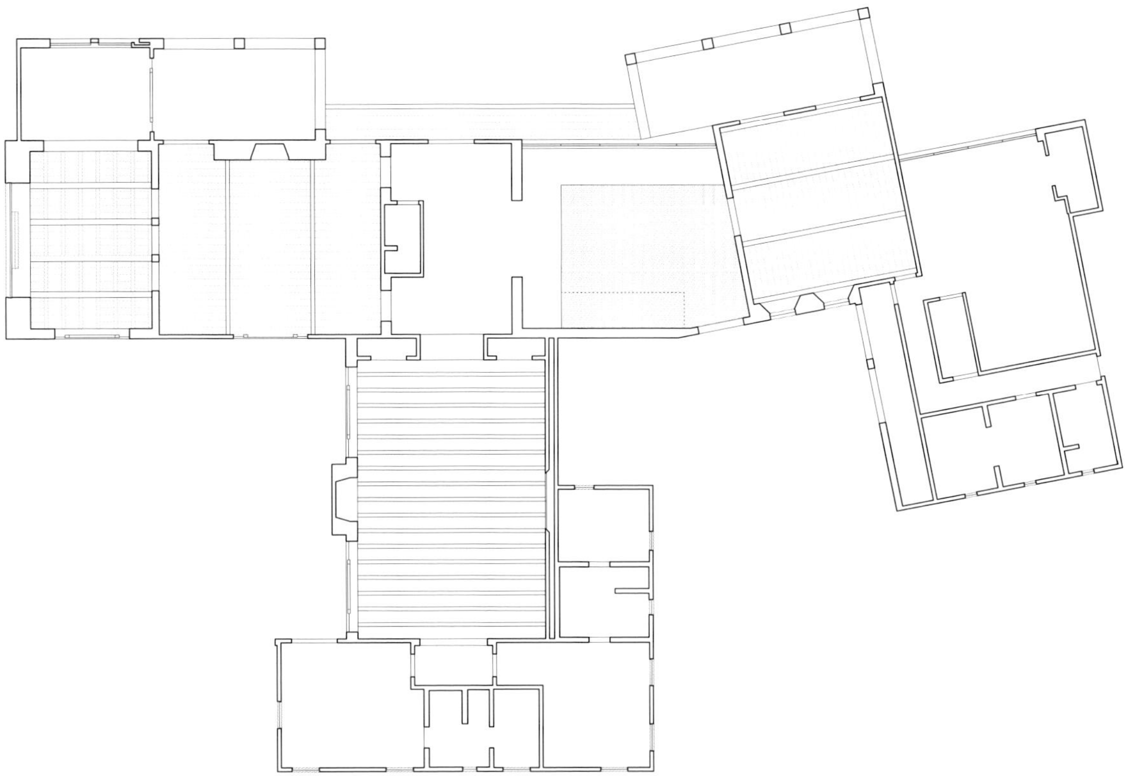

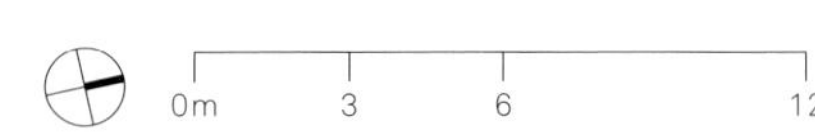

Reflected ceiling plan

Entry foyer Wet bar Master bathroom

Cross sections

Entry foyer

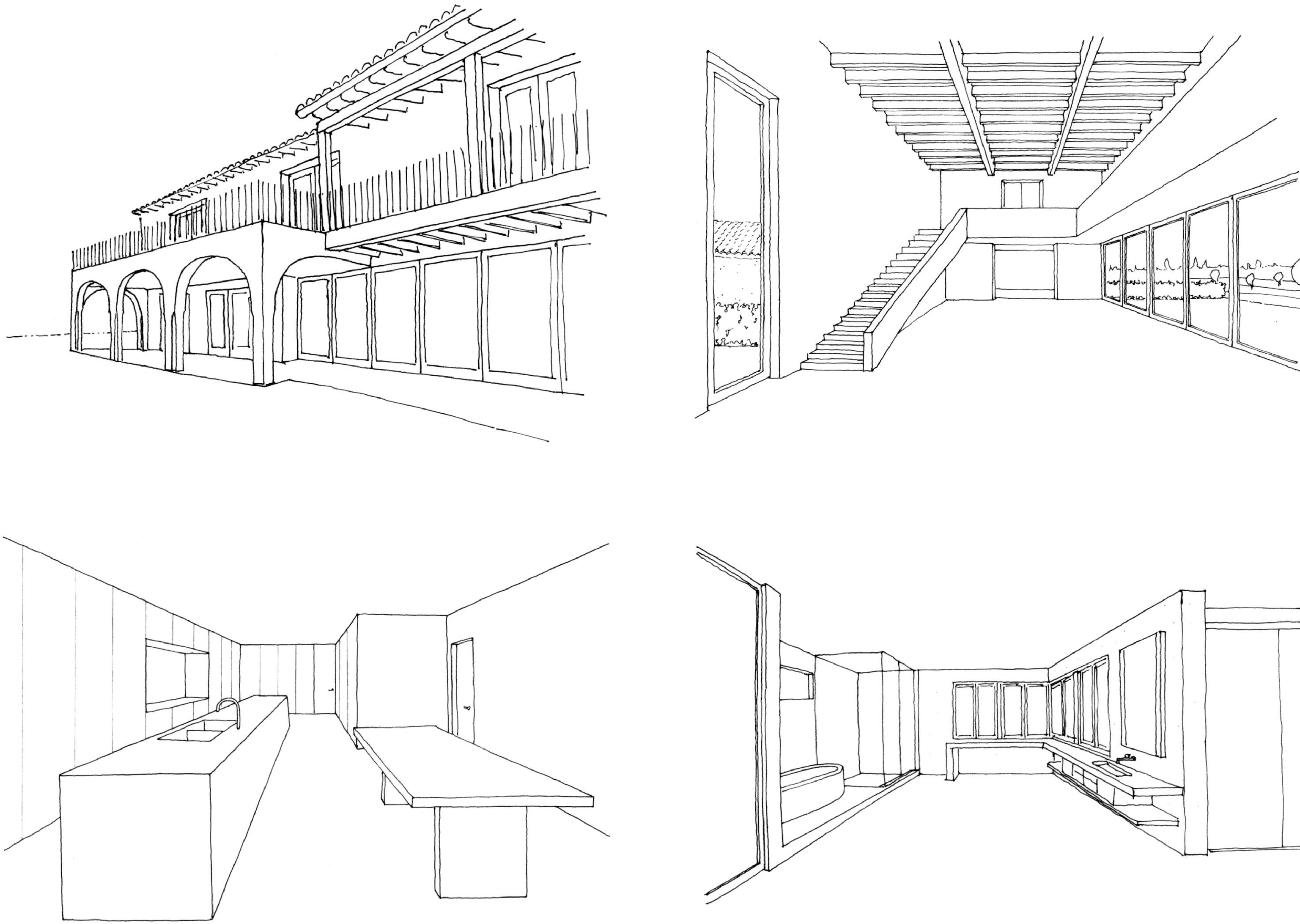

Passage

Family room

Family room

Wet bar

West facade

GALLERIES

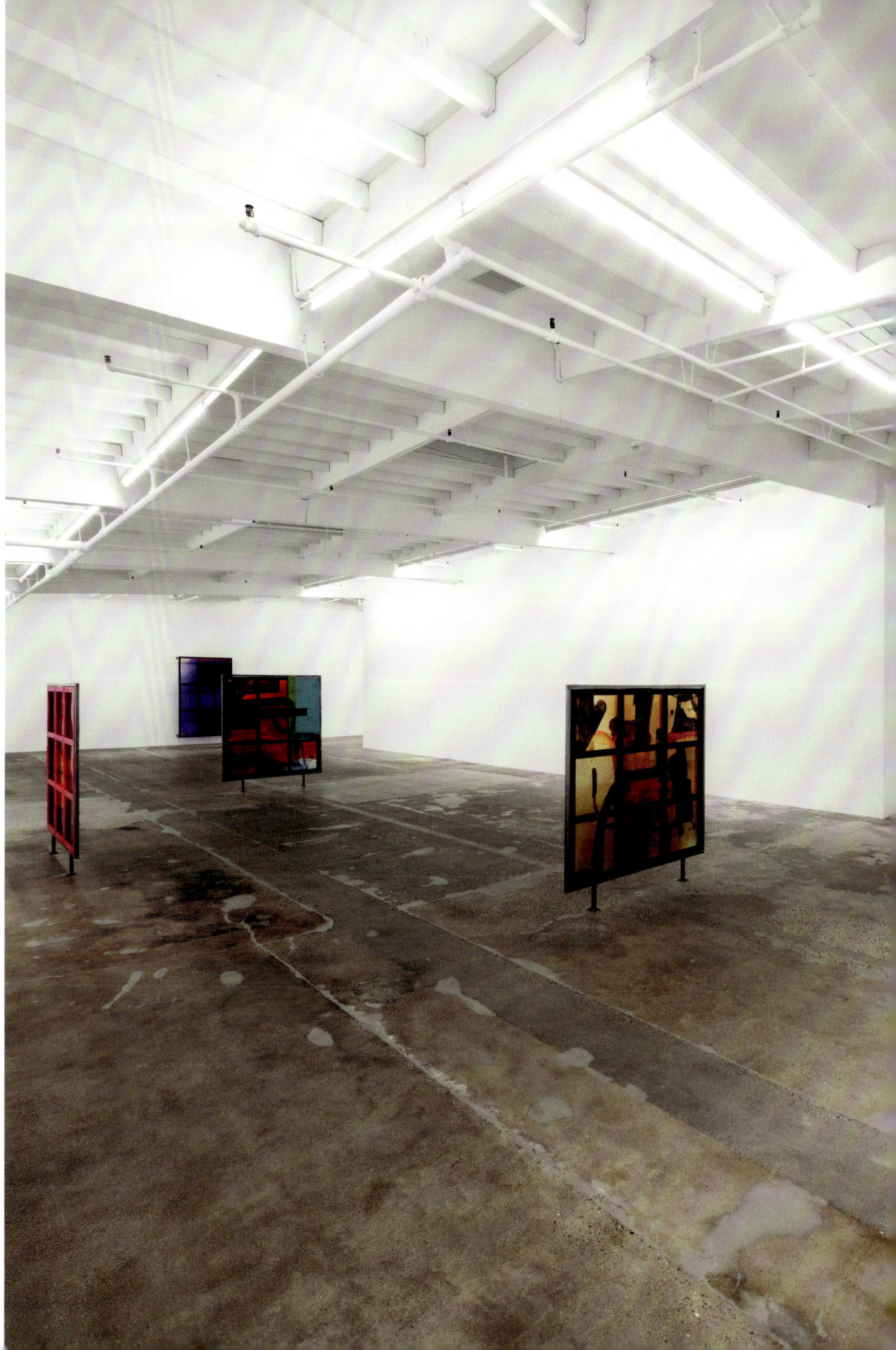

HILLSIDE GALLERY

Santa Monica, 2009

This 2,000 square foot private art gallery in a Santa Monica hillside home maximizes the potential of 'leftover' space. Sandwiched between the sloping hillside below, and an overpass-like concrete deck above, the project challenged Standard to create a cohesive gallery in unusual circumstances.

To make best use of the space available, the gallery is organized on two levels. The entrance to the gallery opens onto a mezzanine space that overlooks the voluminous main gallery below. From the upper level, a wide stairway leads down toward a large north-facing window with a view over the distant landscape.

An undulating ceiling was designed to unify and resolve the abrupt level changes created by the massive concrete structure overhead. The ceiling's white beams emphasize the smooth topography and conceal lighting, mechanical and audiovisual devices.

Rift sawn oak paneling in the lower gallery establishes a horizontal datum, and the same wood is used for the stairway and mezzanine floor. As the ceiling rises, the paneling gives way to white walls, which are complemented by the lower gallery's smooth concrete floors.

Site plan

Bar and entry

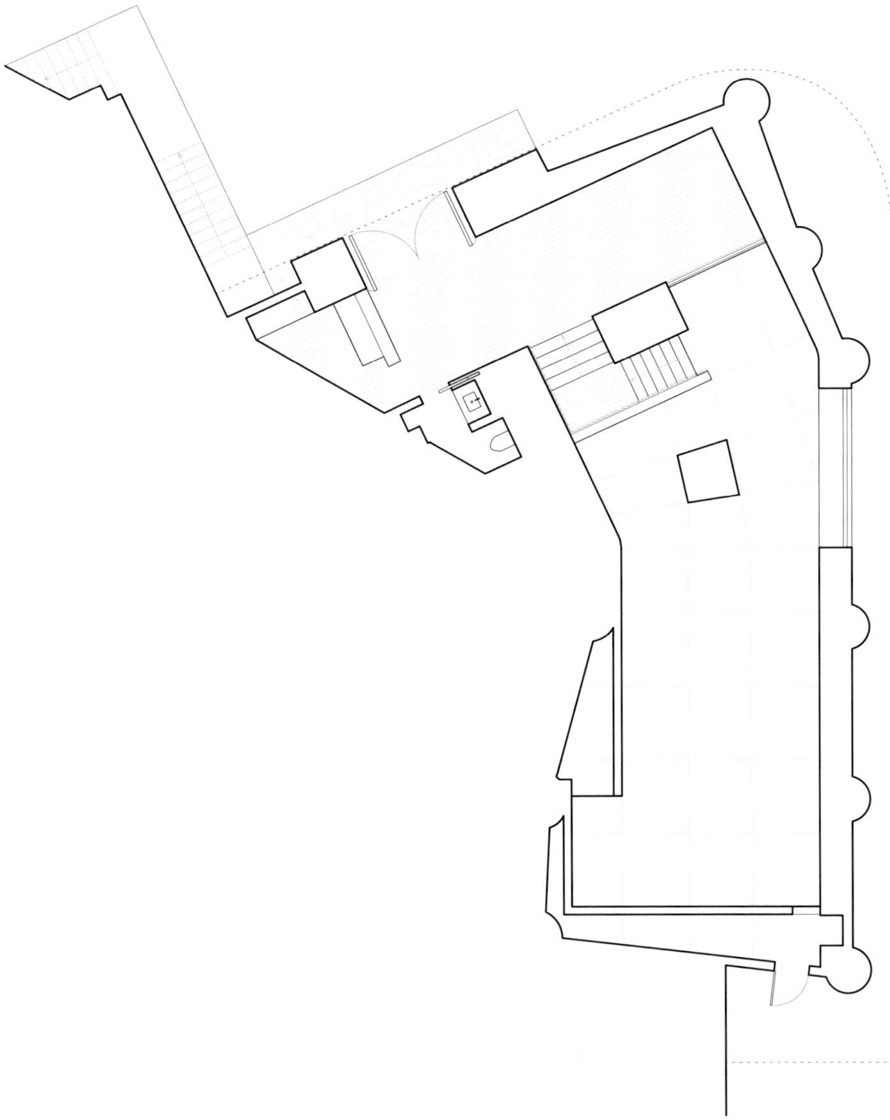

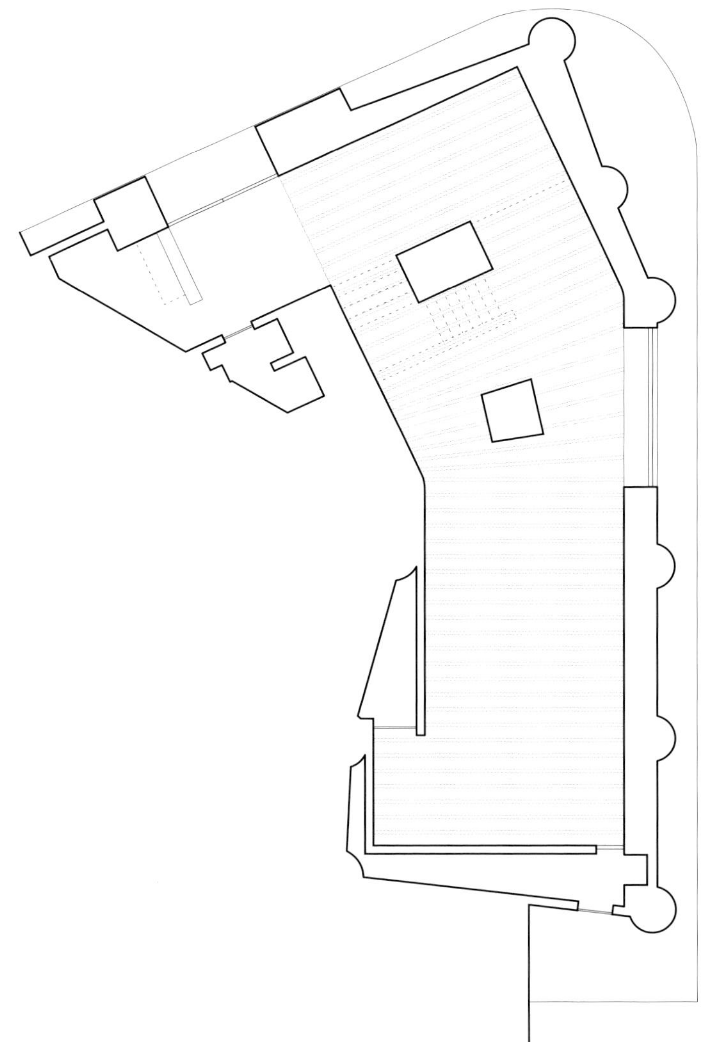

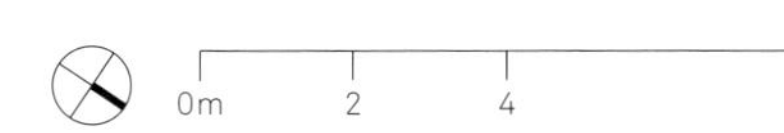

Floor plan

Reflected ceiling plan

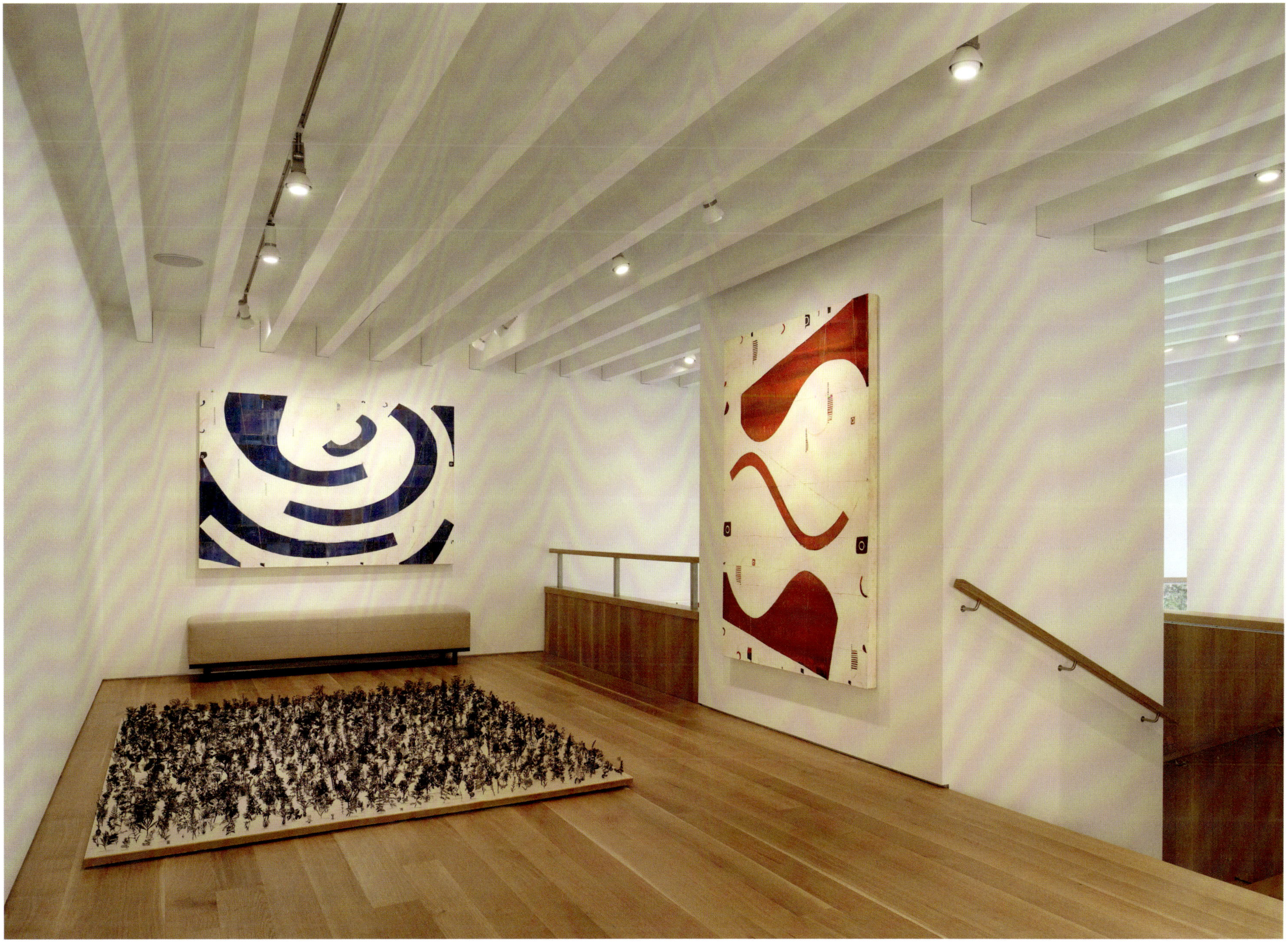

Upper gallery level

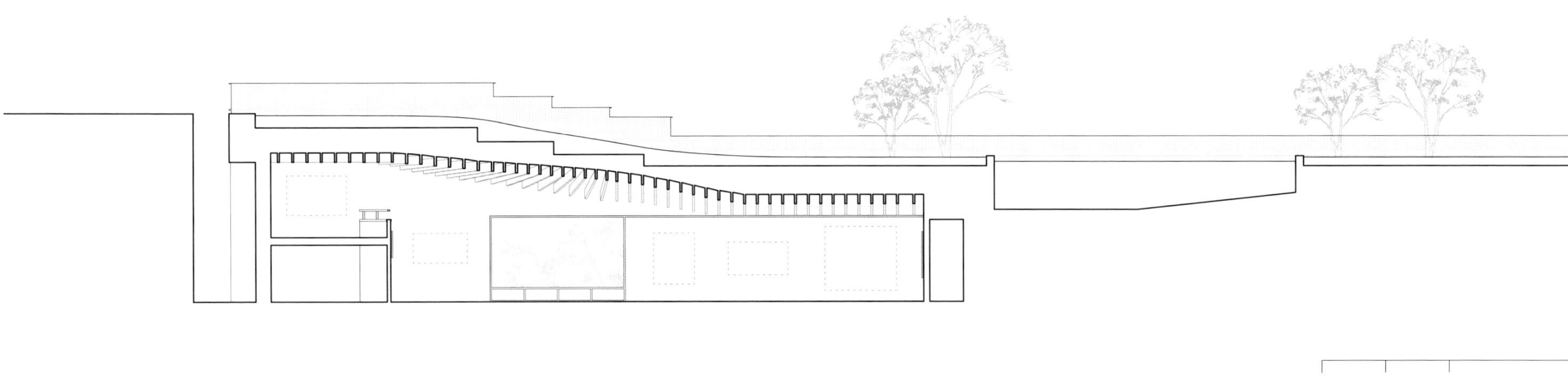

Longitudinal section

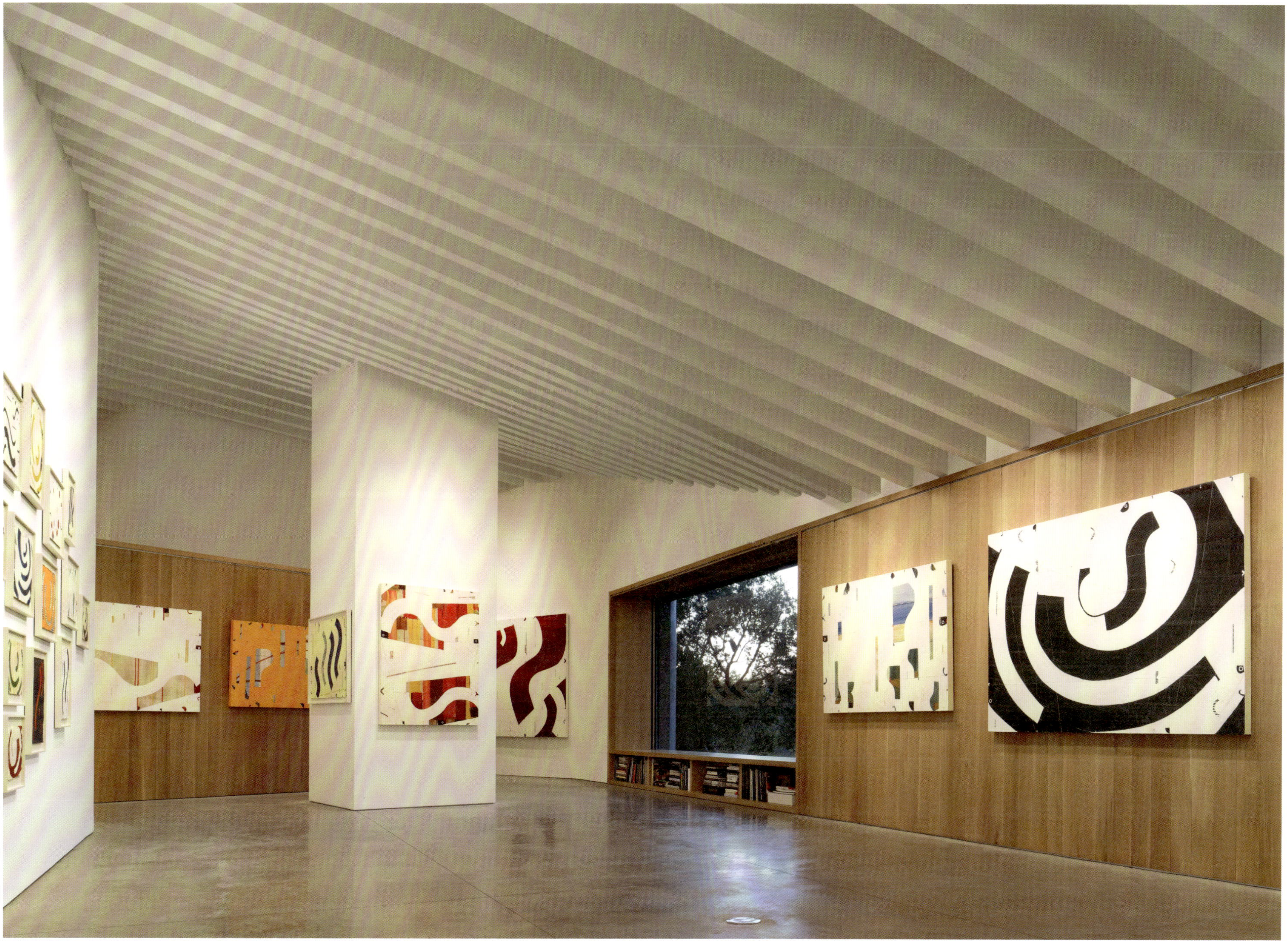

Lower gallery level

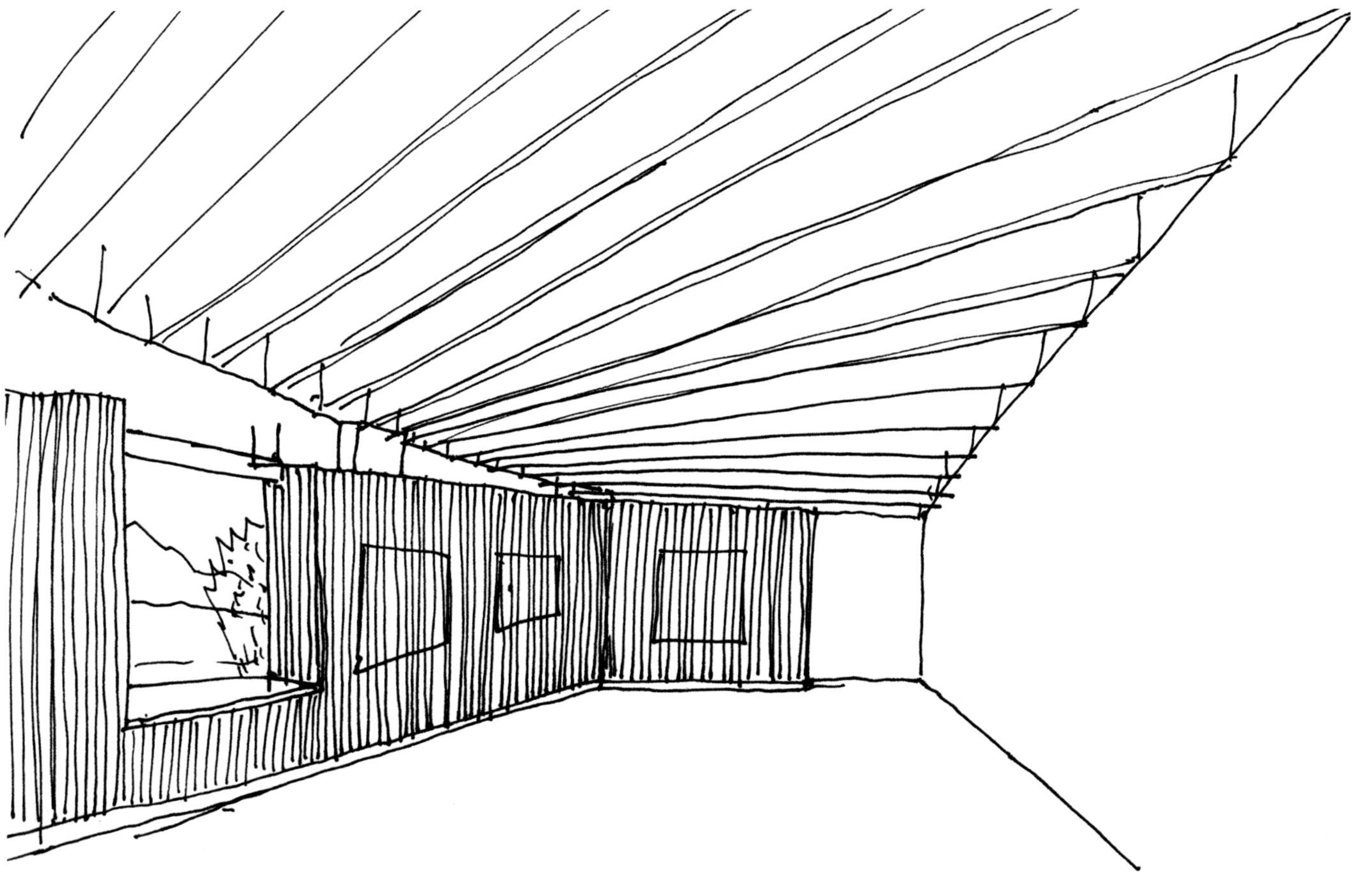

Perspective study

Connecting stair

View of lower gallery

KAYNE GRIFFIN CORCORAN GALLERY

Los Angeles, 2013

At Kayne Griffin Corcoran, the design of the 10,000-square-foot art gallery transforms a typical bow-string truss warehouse and former parking lot into a museum-like gallery space, separated from busy La Brea Avenue, with a landscaped sculpture garden.

The organization of the new exhibition spaces follows the rhythm of the former industrial building's existing structural system, a series of four long span wood trusses supporting the roof, forming a grid above the floor. The grid was used to organize the galleries below, and to inform the ceiling's design. In the main gallery space, pyramidal coffers were formed between the trusses. Topped with skylights and reaching a height of 25 feet, the coffers animate the main gallery with natural light. In the ancillary galleries, ceiling heights are maximized at 15 feet at the bottom cords of the trusses. Large steel and glass pivot doors were designed to open the galleries to the entry courtyard, making a gracious indoor–outdoor connection that facilitates receptions.

The gallery's street entrance is a high steel gate between tall hedges, leading to a walled garden. The building's former asphalt parking area was converted to a landscaped forecourt, with grass paving and a raised terrace covered by a steel trellis. The existing brick exterior walls were covered in creeping fig, and the plantings were retained and preserved during construction. The green walls, combined with the grass floor, make the large entry courtyard an oasis and a buffer from busy La Brea Boulevard outside.

In addition to a James Turrell-designed, permanent "Skyspace" room featuring a retractable roof, the skylights of the public galleries are covered with a translucent scrim that is backlit with programmable LED lighting, enabling the main gallery spaces to be transformed with color.

Site plan

Main gallery

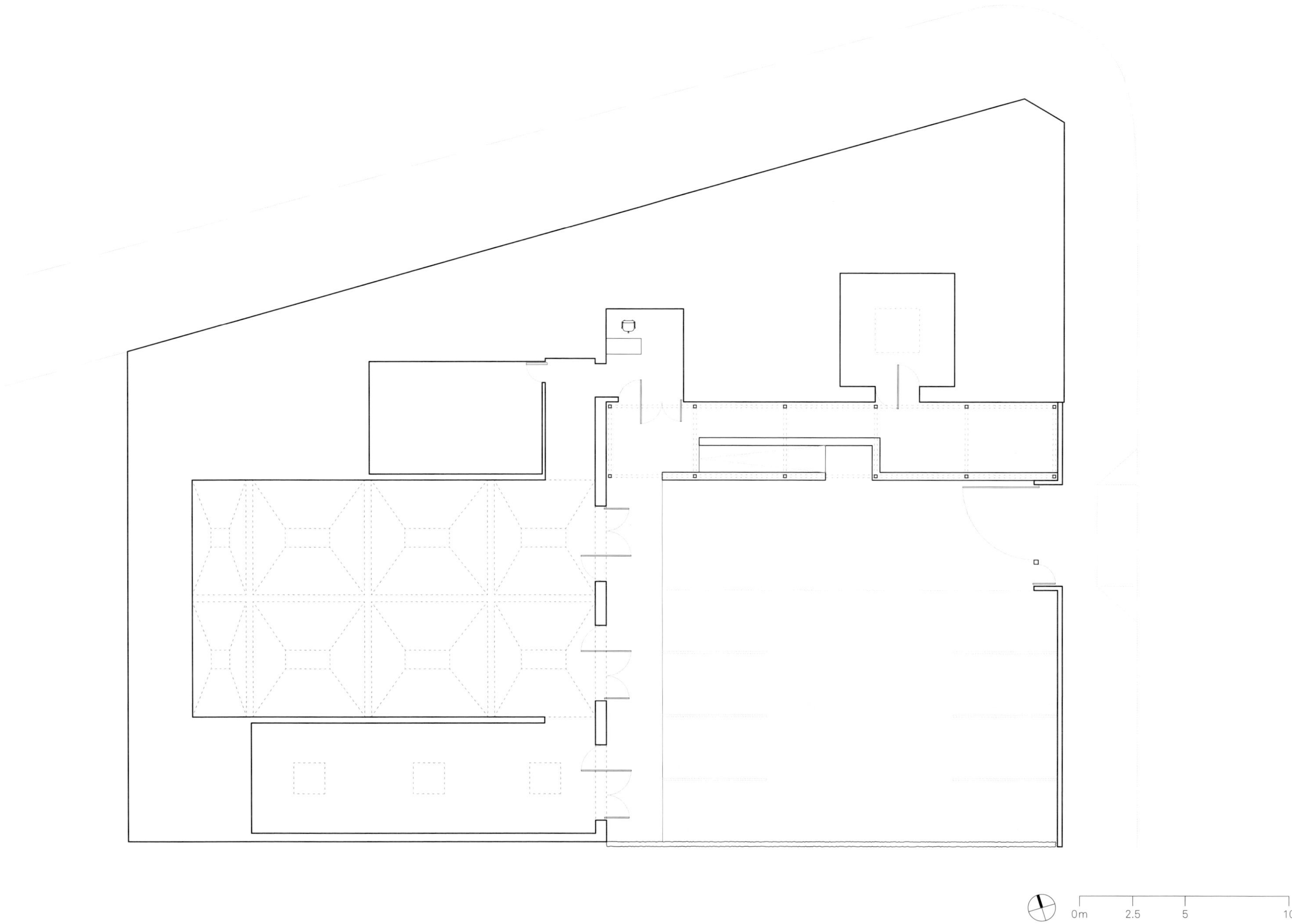

Floor plan

Main gallery

Secondary gallery

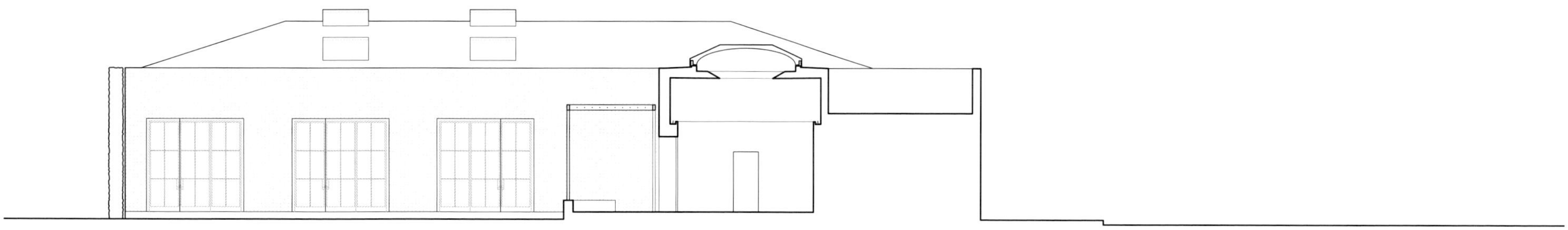

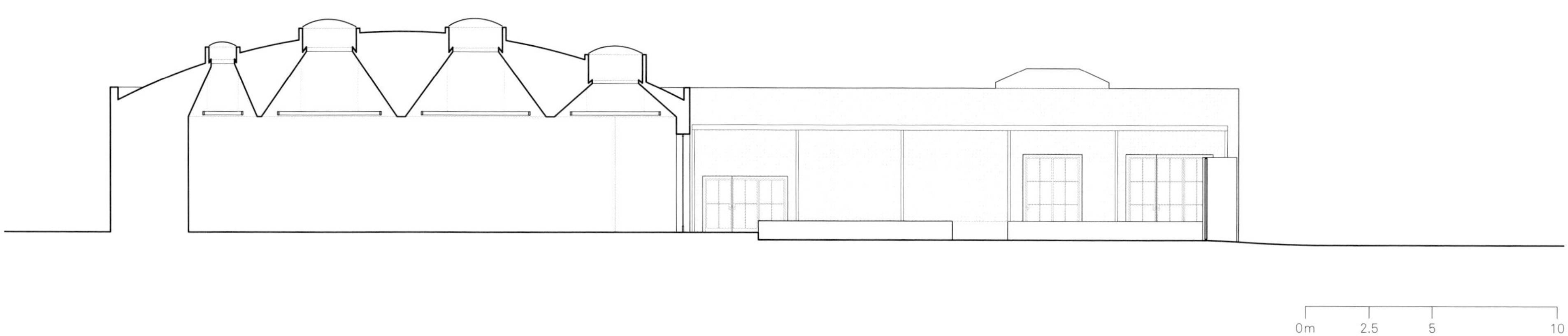

Longitudinal section

Cross section

Main gallery Courtyard

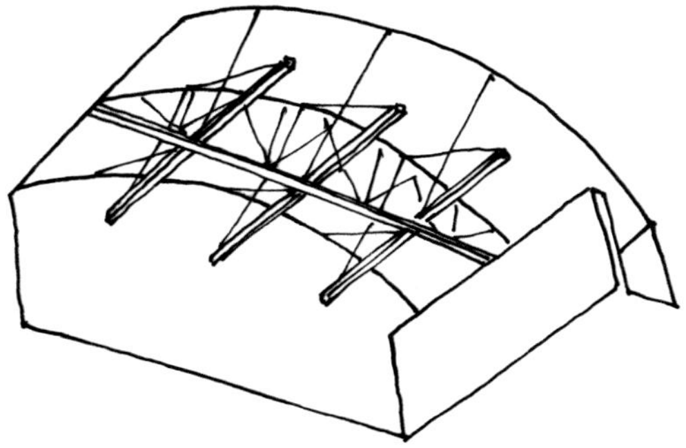

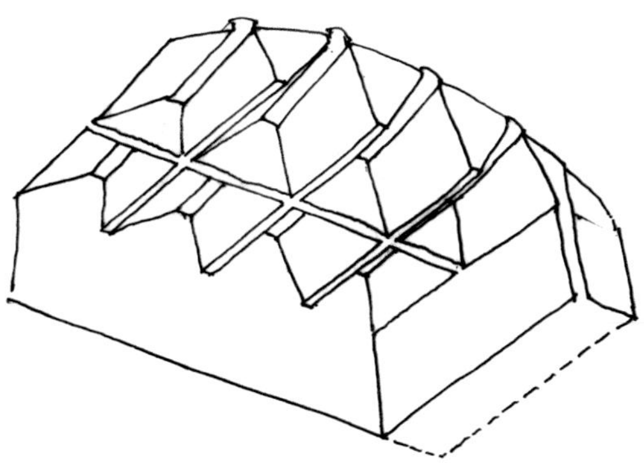

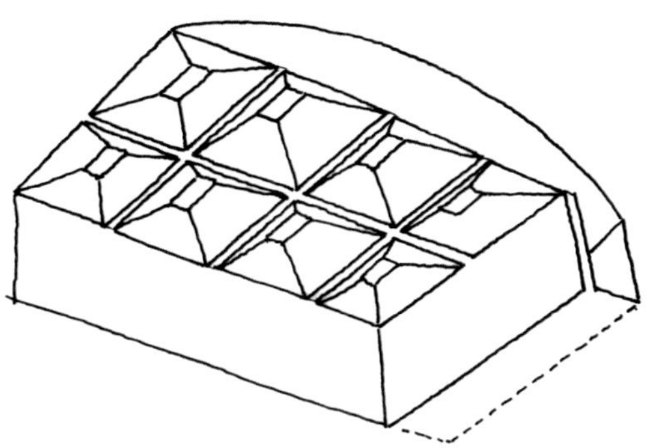

Main gallery

Pivot doors to courtyard

MACCARONE GALLERY

Los Angeles, 2015

For the Los Angeles outpost of this New York-based contemporary art gallery, Standard was asked to transform a warehouse building and its adjacent outdoor spaces into a 32,000-square-foot complex of exhibition spaces, artists' studios and project rooms.

The east and west warehouses were repurposed as artist studios, and they retain their raw industrial character. The central 12,000 -square-foot warehouse has been transformed into a gallery space. A vacant railway to the south of the warehouses functions as an entry court and sculpture garden for the exhibition space.

Because the warehouse floors are several feet above the street, a long sloping concrete walk leads to a level platform at the entrance doors. The raised platform resembles the loading docks common to the area, and is lined with an industrial metal guardrail. The unpainted brick exterior walls of the buildings were not altered, and the steel entry doors were inserted into the existing openings. The metal meshes used for the gates and guardrails are typical of the industrial character of the Arts District area. The surface of the vacant railway is covered in gray decomposed granite, recalling the crushed stone ballast found under the nearby rail tracks.

Inside the gallery, the design approach was to create an uninterrupted exhibition surface. A U-shaped exhibition wall lines the perimeter of the warehouse, and wraps around a central partition. The south wall of the space was left as brick, and is punctuated by the entry doors and the reception desk.

The gallery is illuminated by a combination of natural daylight and LED lighting, providing an even radiance. Because the gallery is primarily visited during the day, natural light is the primary light source. Translucent skylights filter light through the white-painted, wood beamed roof, reflecting daylight throughout the gallery. Rows of LED lights are mounted to the roof beams, lining the walls, supplementing the natural light and washing the walls with a continuous glow.

Site plan

EXIT

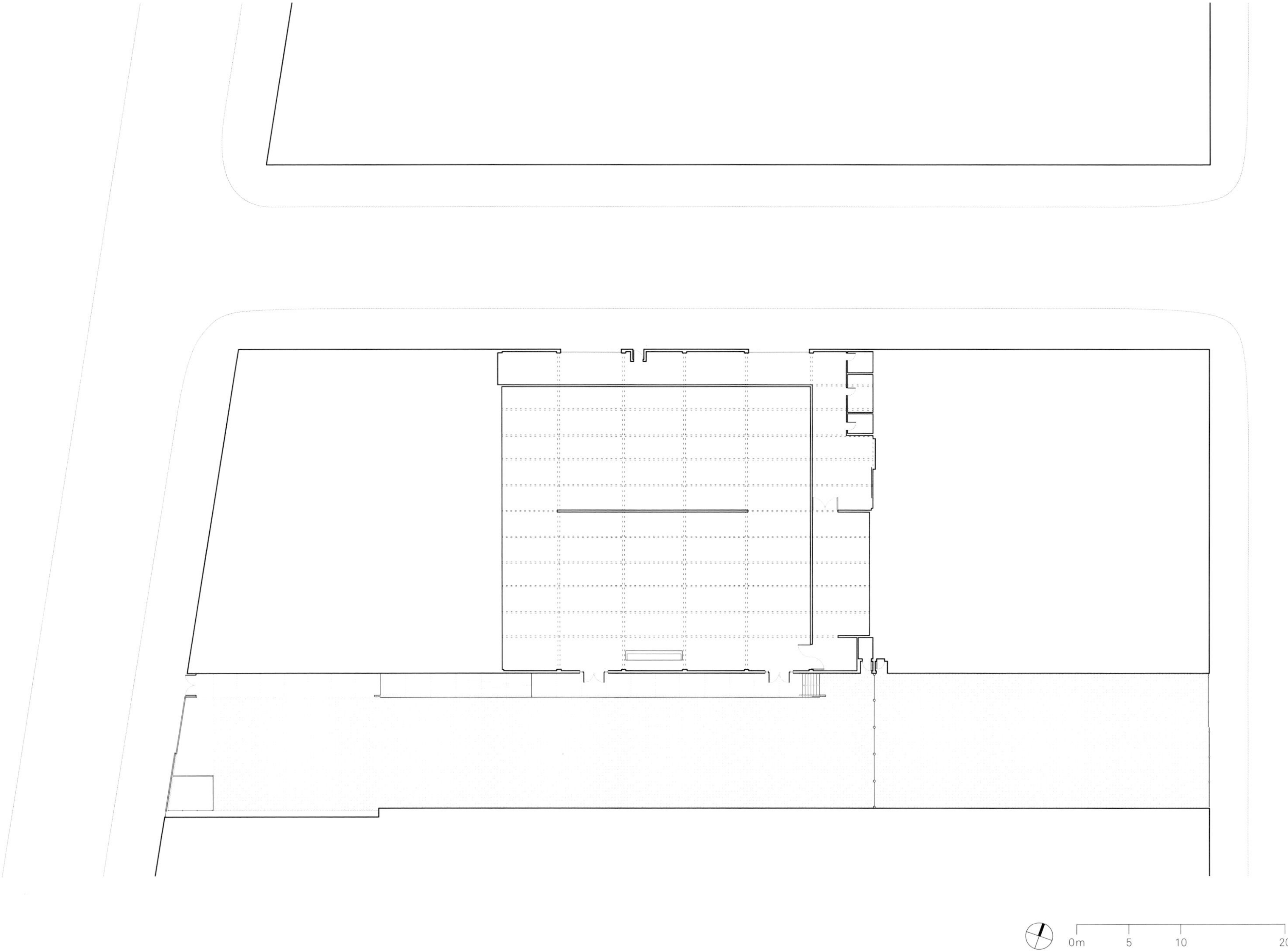

Floor plan

Entry doors

Perimeter wall

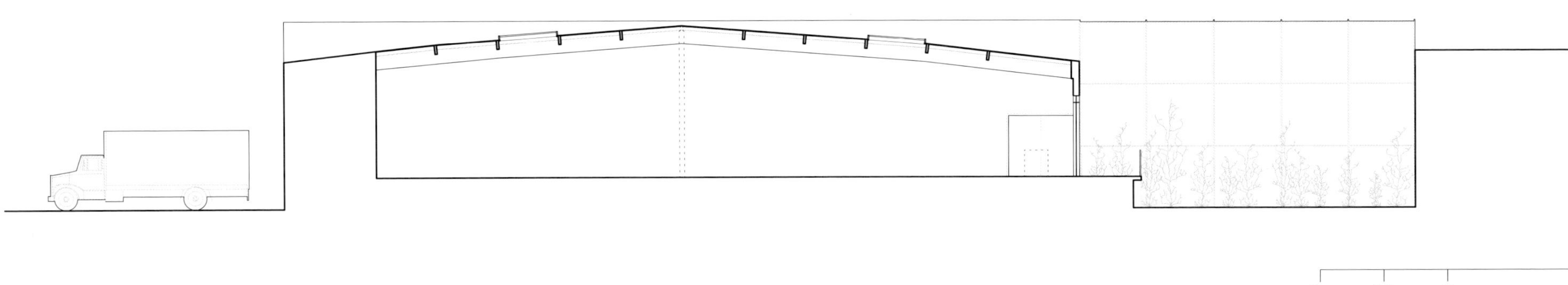

Cross section

Views of gallery

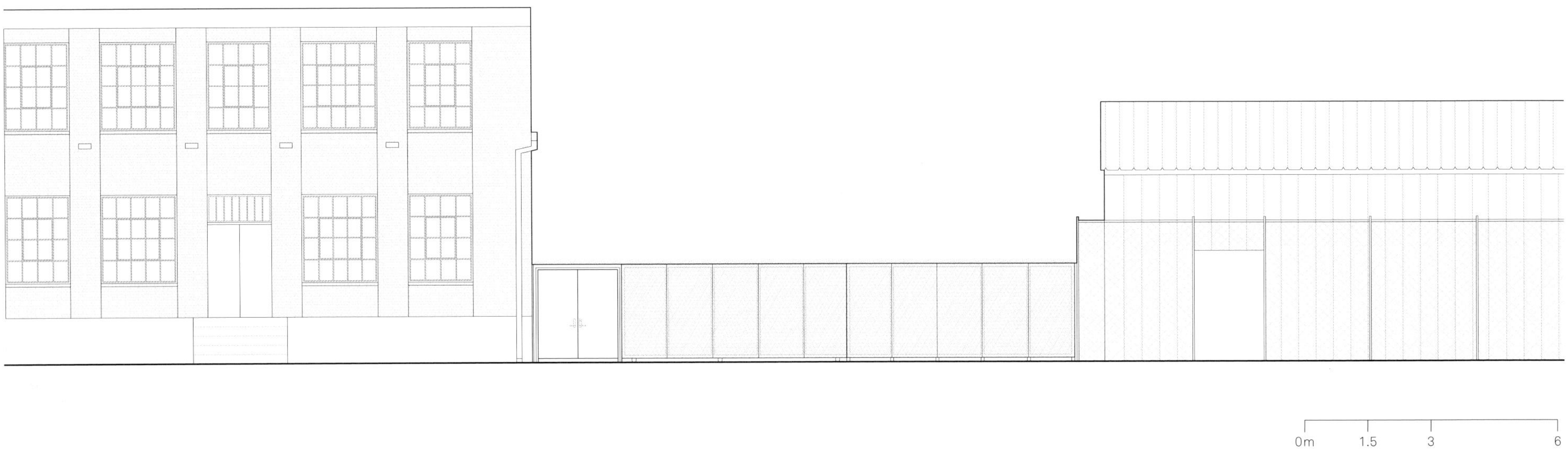

Street elevation

Entry gate

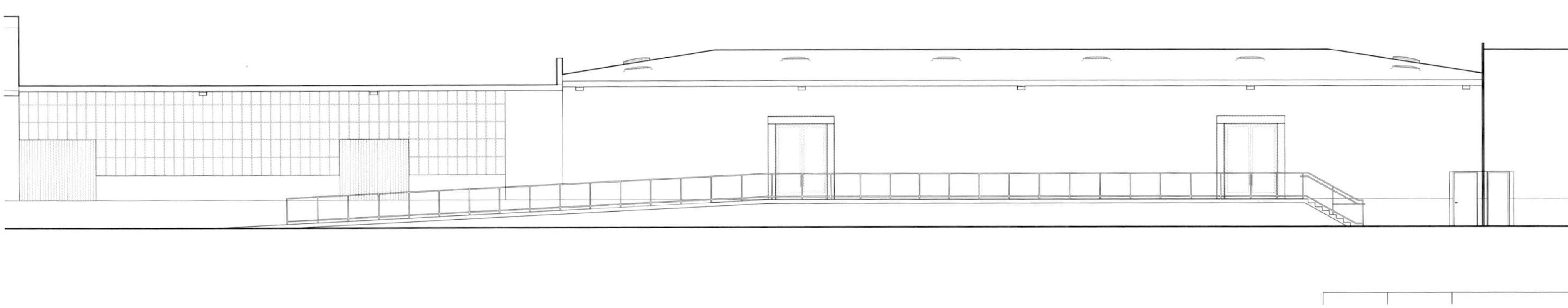

Courtyard elevation

Entry ramp

Sculpture garden

Perpendicular view at night

Diagonal view at night

Entry doors and ramp

Entry doors

RETAIL

JAMES PERSE STORE

Los Angeles, 2003

The original James Perse Store, on Melrose Avenue, takes advantage of the existing building's domestic scale and structural columns to create a linear plan that amplifies the depth of the space.

The design works around a row of structural columns, concealing and transforming them into a delineation between two major retail zones that are differentiated through contrasting materials: the men's clothing space uses maple furniture on a concrete floor, while the area for women and children's clothing is defined by white lacquered displays, on an oak floor. The existing sloping wood ceiling was sandblasted and a soffit was suspended to unify the space.

California's light and climate are welcomed into the store through skylights and a 30-foot-wide sliding glass door, which opens to an outdoor seating area and bamboo garden. The building's existing skylights were reglazed with white glass to diffuse the light, and new skylights were added to add a wash of soft light to walls along the spine of the store.

Site plan

Storefront

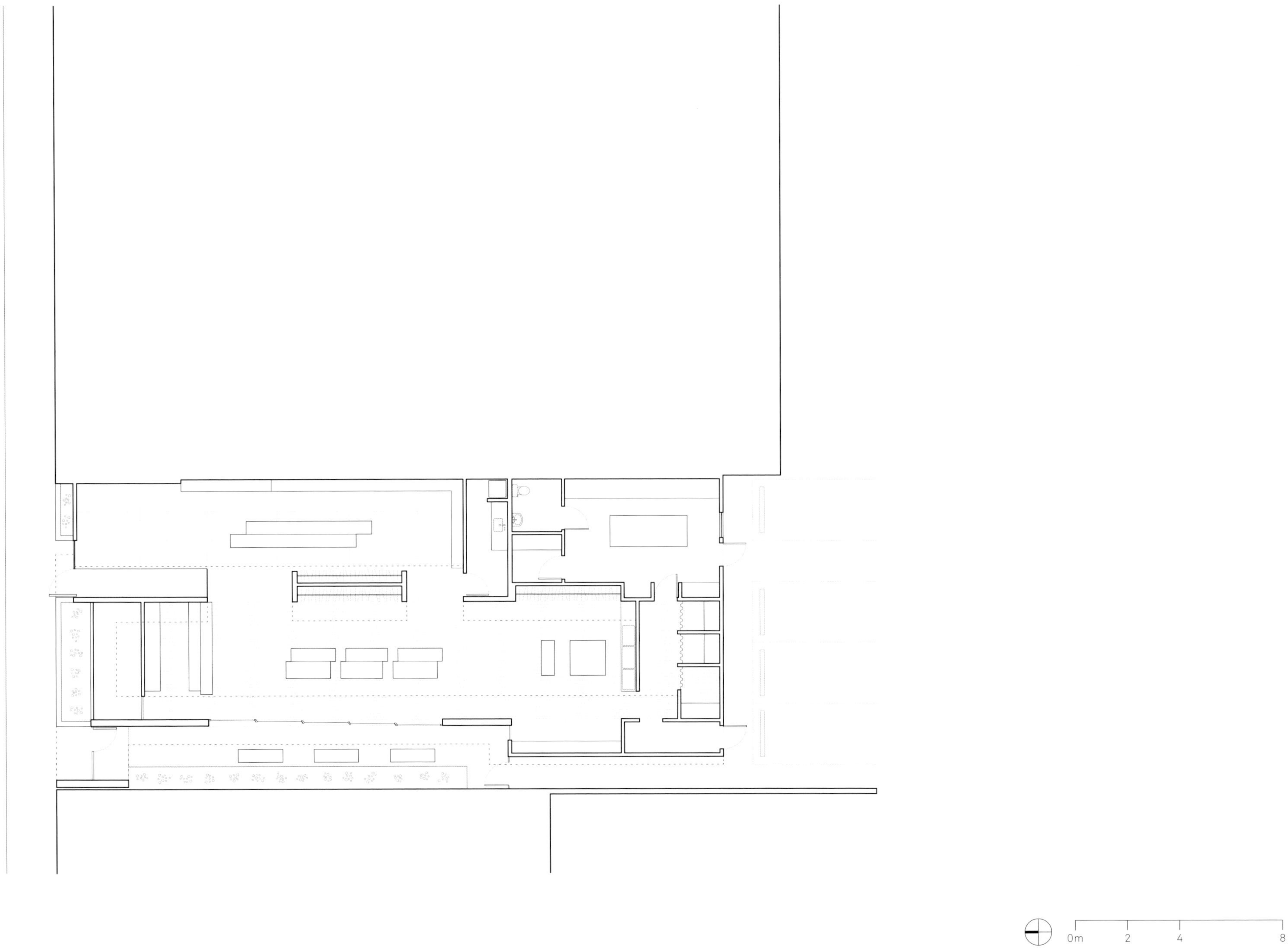

Floor plan

Men's sales area

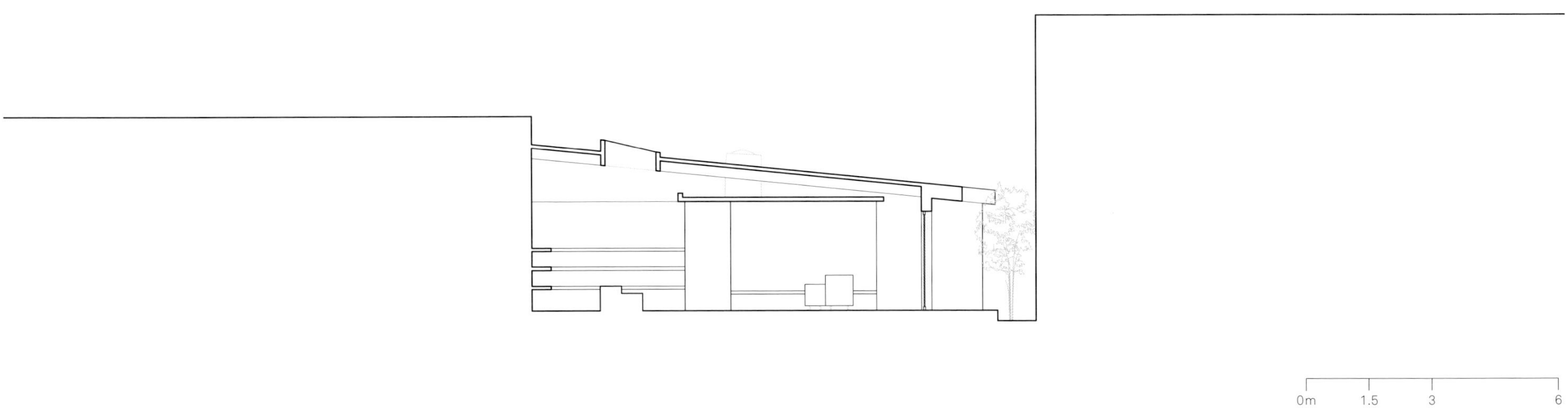

Cross section

View to men's sales area

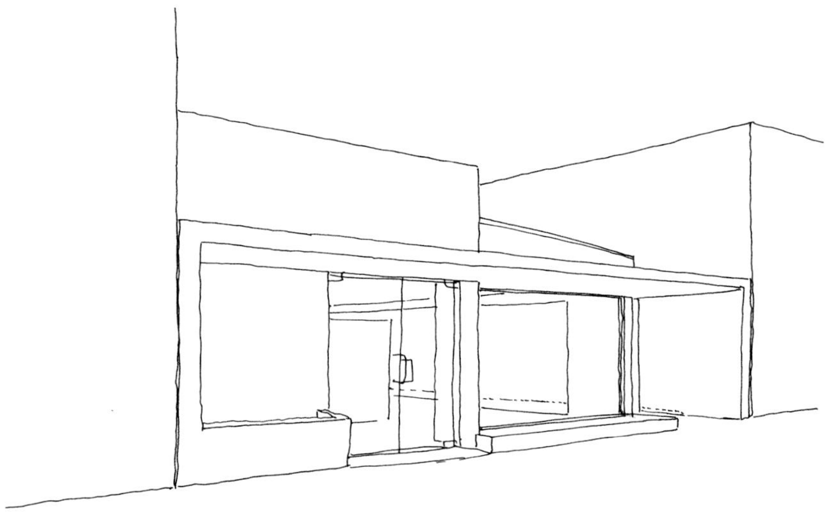

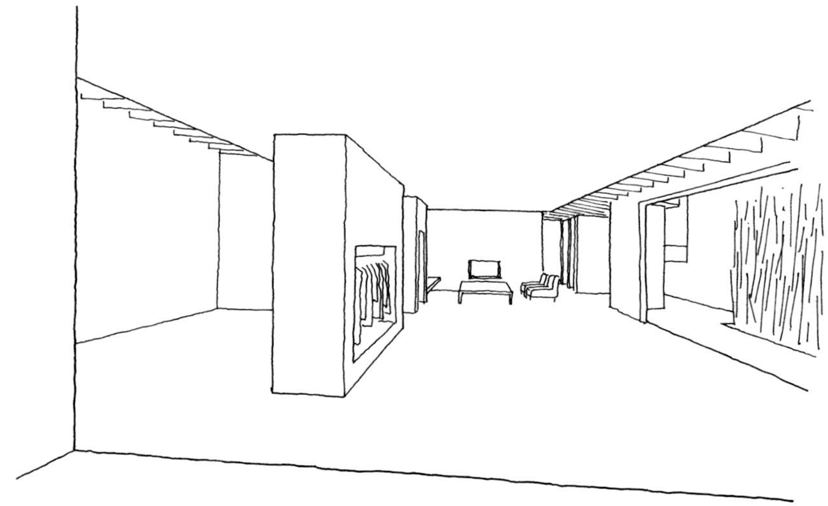

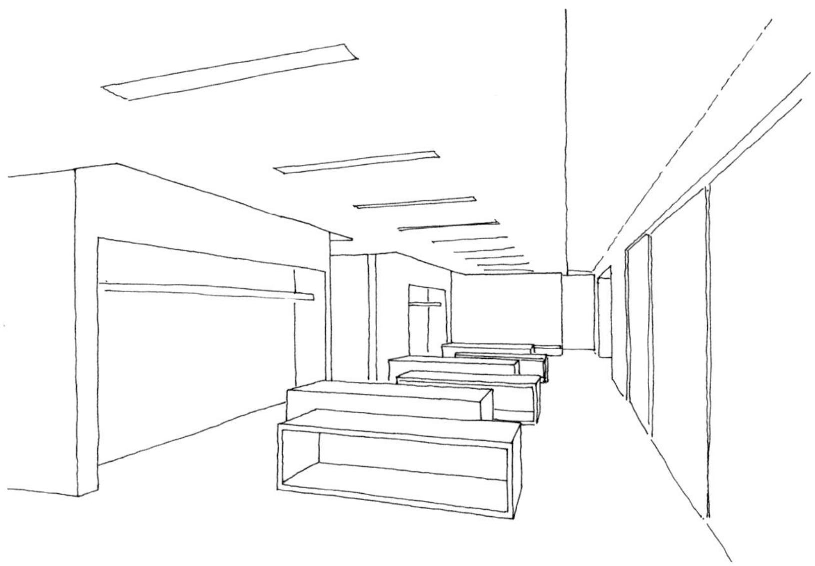

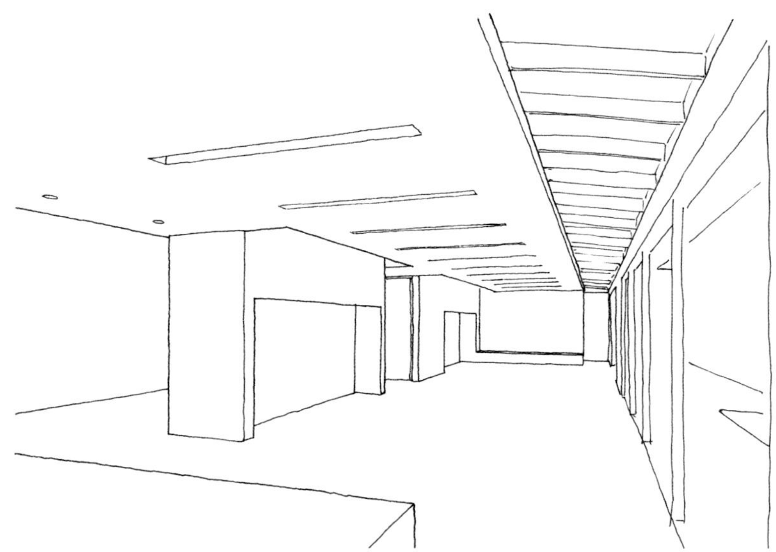

Women's sales area

Women's sales area

JAMES PERSE

JAMES PERSE STORE

Beverly Hills, 2007

The bold but minimal facade of the flagship store transforms the north end of sleepy Canon Drive. Standard's design radically altered the existing two-story building to create a new storefront that confidently announces the arrival of the store. With its attention to detail, proportion and materials, the design maintains continuity with previous James Perse stores while accommodating the growth of Perse's luxury label.

Floor-to-ceiling sliding teak shutter doors and a recessed second story loggia distinguish the facade from adjacent retail stores and restaurants. The shutters slide horizontally to reveal or conceal the long shop window and entrance. Functioning as a transitional zone, like a portico in a classical palazzo, this protected entry space merges the inside and outside, public and private.

The store's fluid plan is organized around a garden courtyard that features a wood deck and olive tree. The boutique captures the comfort of a southern California domestic setting by blurring the boundaries between indoor and outdoor spaces, and making generous use of natural light and elemental wood, stone, plaster and glass. The shutter-veiled storefront is echoed by the courtyard trellis and pivoting glass doors opening to it. This project established the design template for subsequent James Perse stores in Malibu and the Hamptons.

Site plan

Storefront

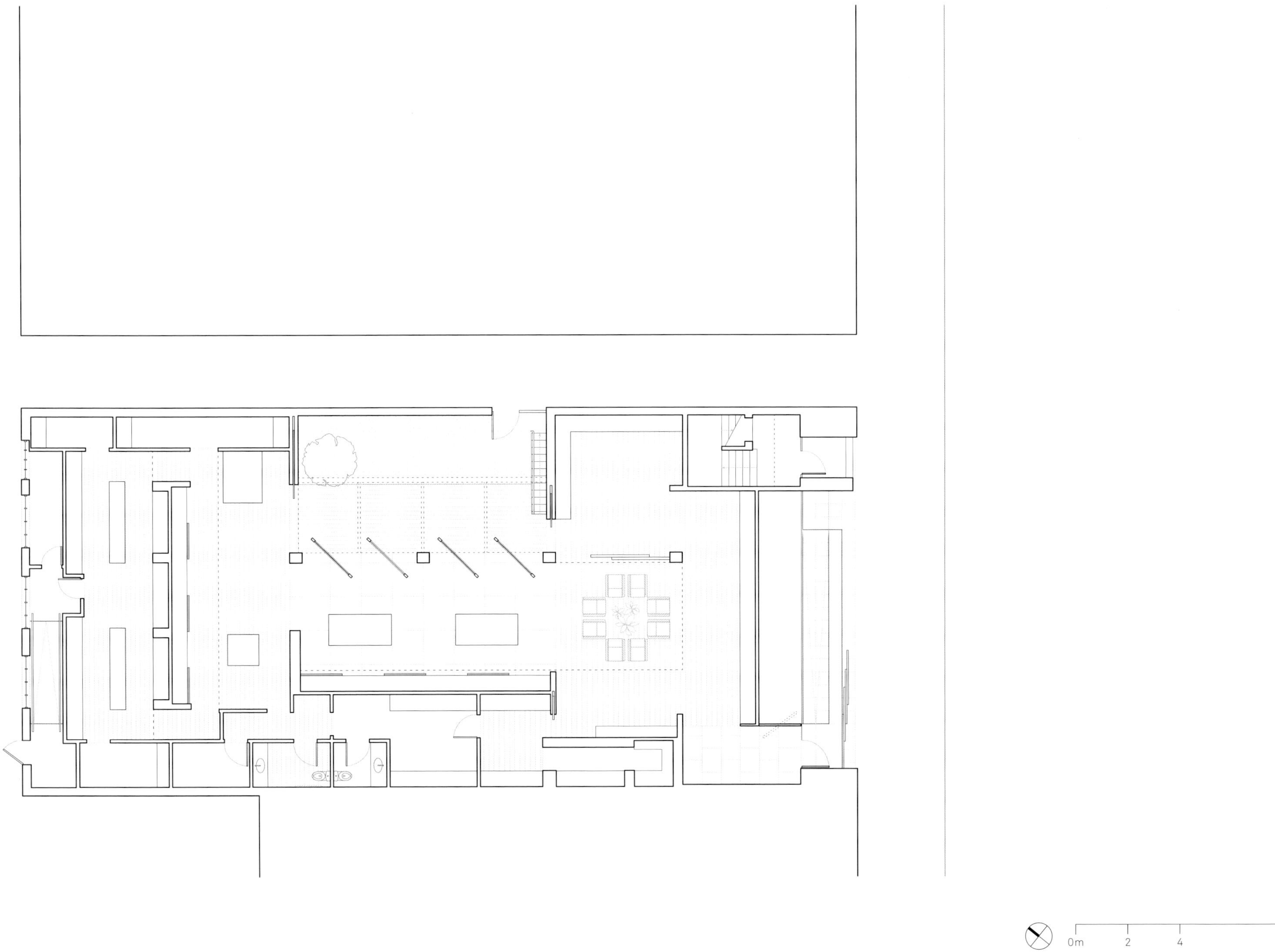

Floor plan

Sales areas

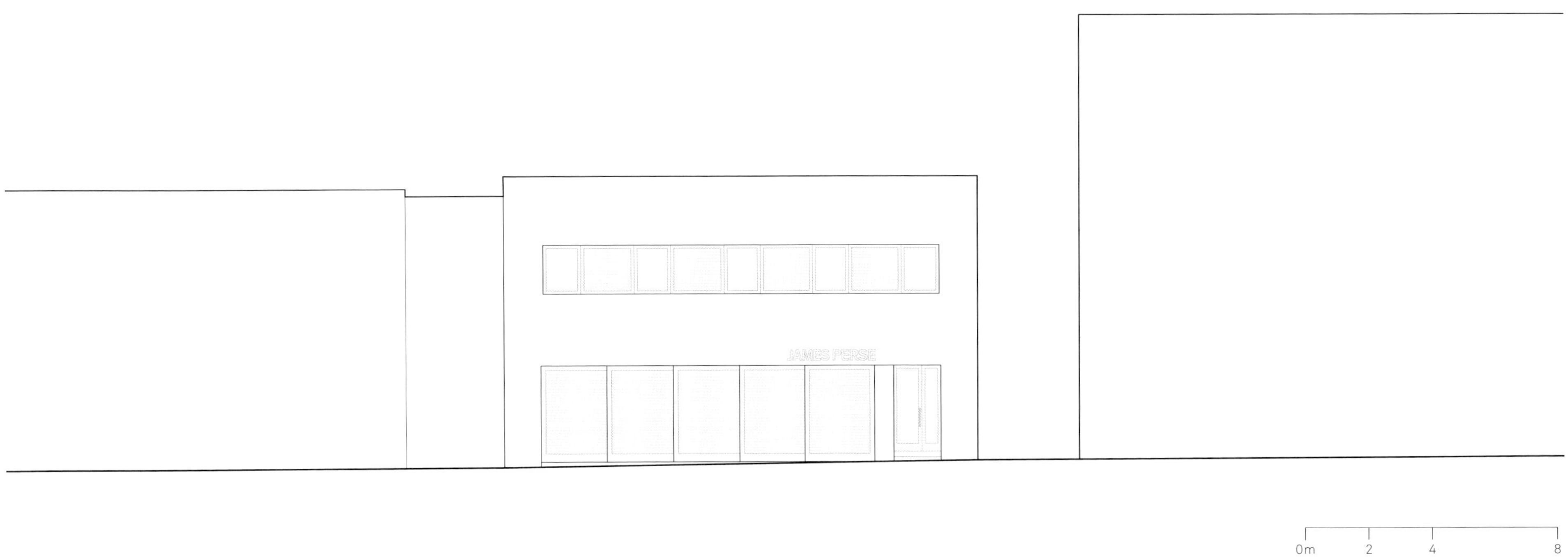

Street elevation

NELSON
SHELTON
REAL ESTATE
JAMES PERSE
NELSON SHELTON REAL ESTATE
Luxe
Classics
Home
Accessories
Kids
Malibu

Storefront

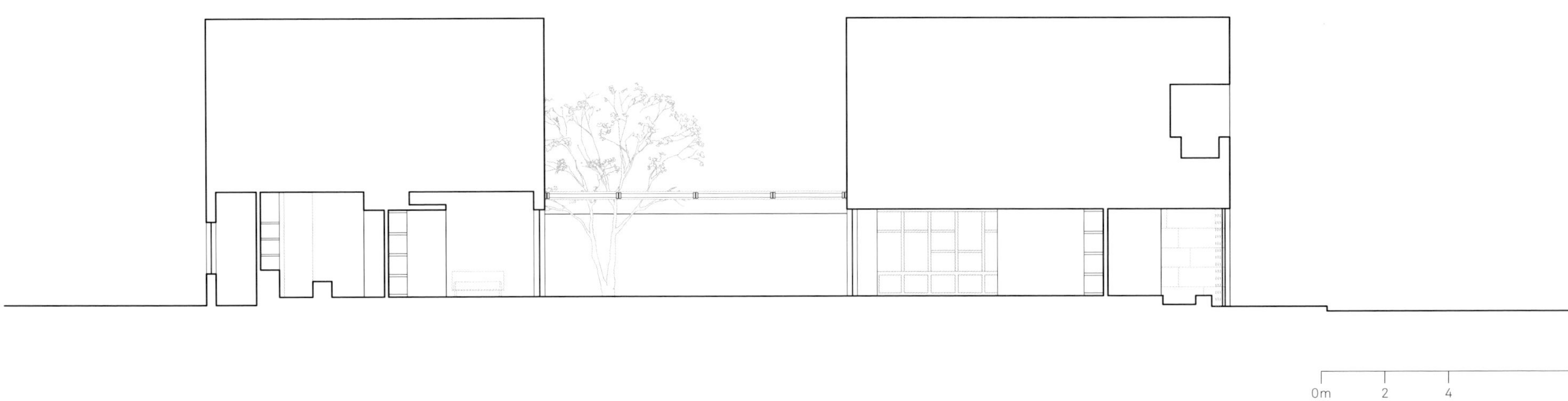

Longitudinal section

Entry ramp

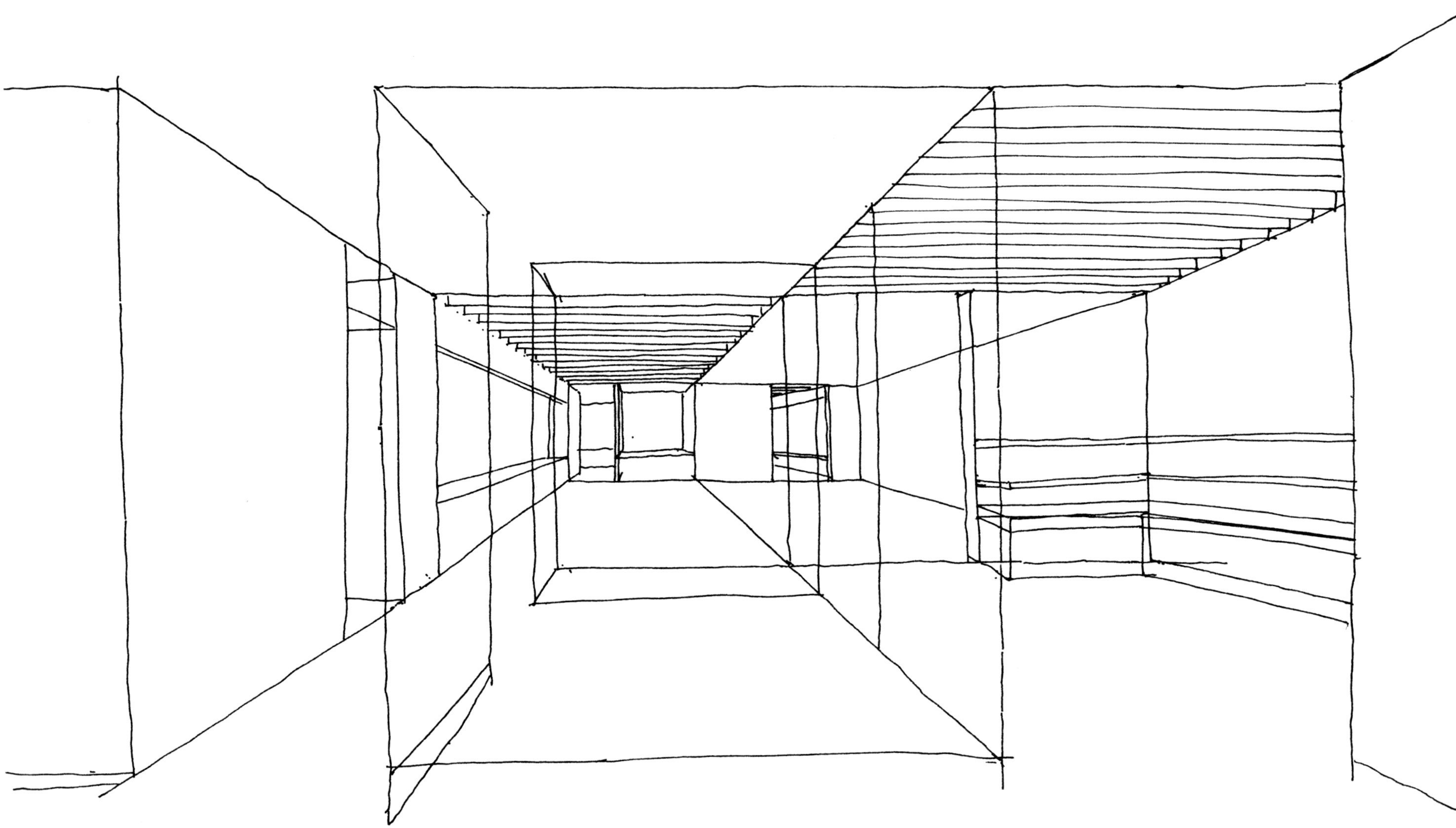

Sales area at entry

NELSON
SHELTON
REAL ESTATE
JAMES PERSE
SHELTON REAL ESTATE

JENNI KAYNE STORE

Los Angeles, 2007

In a West Hollywood neighborhood of art galleries, fashion designer Jenni Kayne's debut boutique is designed to combine the clarity and openness of a gallery setting with the comfort of a California home. The former warehouse space was transformed via a series of sustainability-minded choices and an aesthetic program that is minimalist and modern yet comfortable.

The boutique boldly announces its presence with a glowing glass corner above a floating display window. Behind iron gates, a vestibule leads through wood-clad doors into the spacious and spare interior of the brick and steel building. Newly constructed interior walls layer the building's 2,400 square feet into a series of light-filled display rooms.

Standard's design ethos and Kayne's desire to make earth-friendly choices aligned in their joint material, component and concept decisions throughout the project, including the use of bamboo casework, recycled cotton insulation, fluorescent lighting and low volatile organic compound (VOC) finishes.

The building's existing materials are salvaged and tied back into the design. Concrete floors, ground and stained black, provide a dramatic backdrop for vitrines of brass, glass and bamboo. Steel beams, left unfinished, combine with new cedar slats to form a canopy over the interior white and wood-paneled walls. Meanwhile, the building's brick perimeter walls have been exposed on the interior and painted white, acknowledging the structure's rough character while softening the space and heightening its luminosity.

Site plan

Storefront

Jenni Kayne

Floor plan

Main sales area

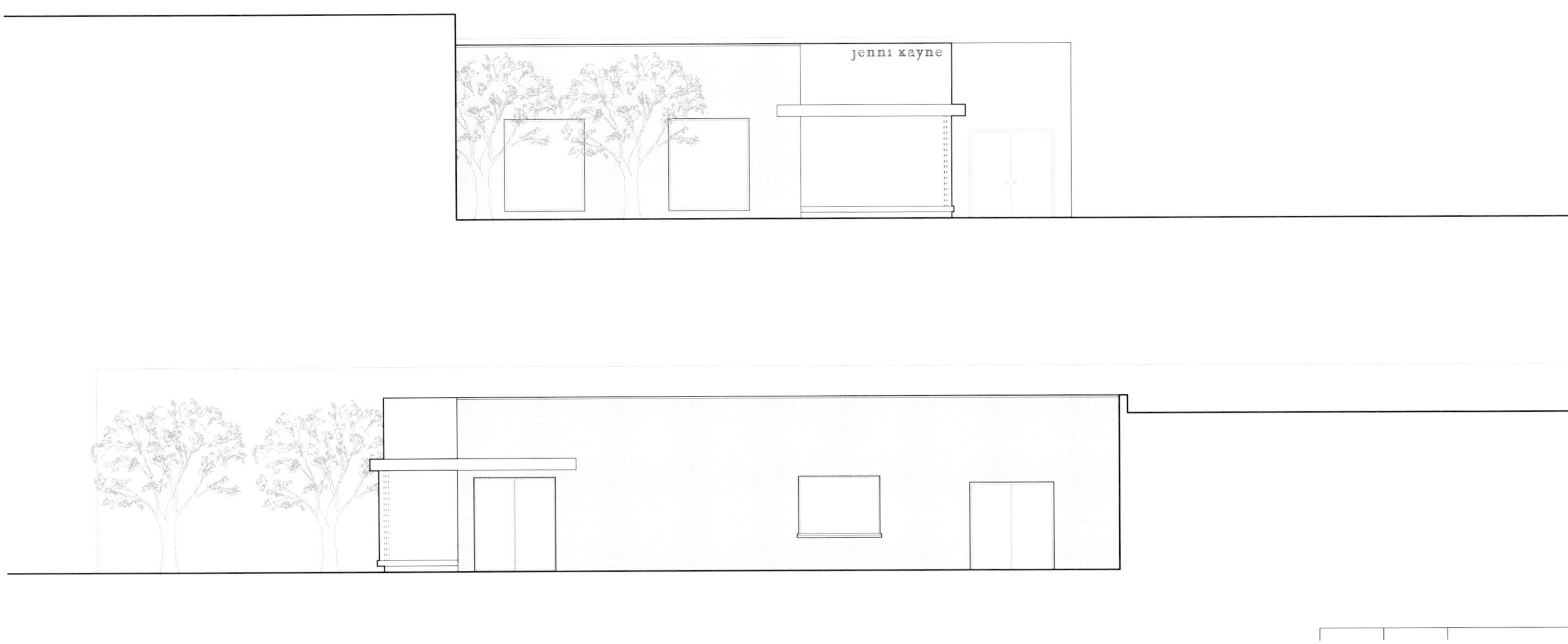

Street elevation Entrance elevation

Storefront

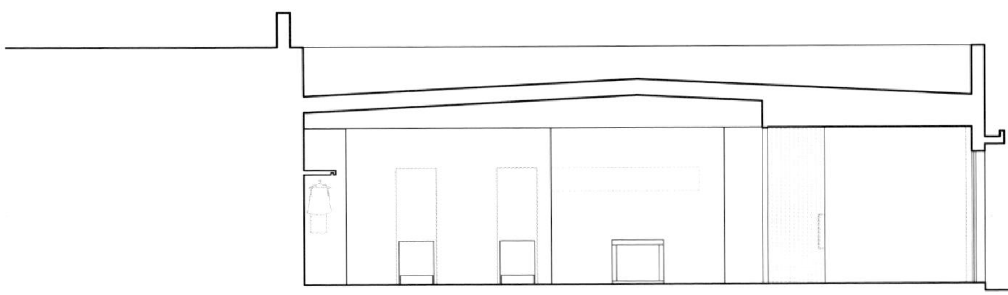

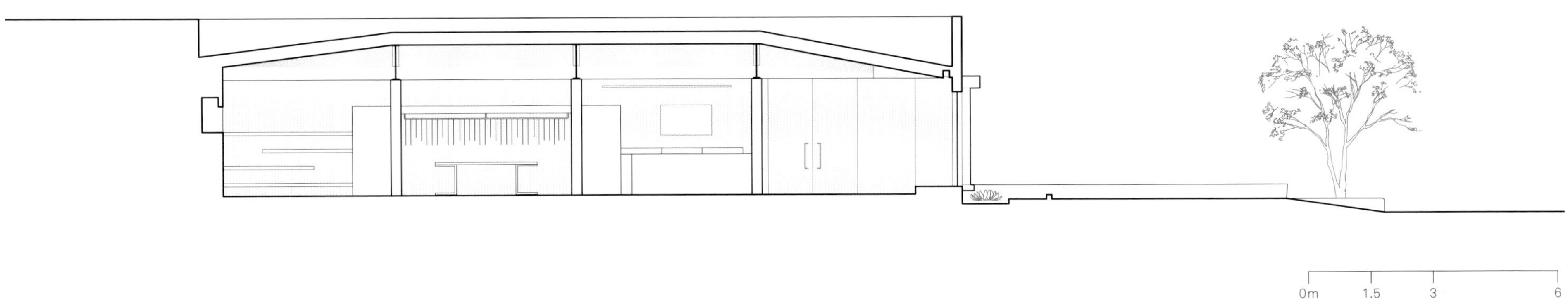

Longitudinal section

Cross section

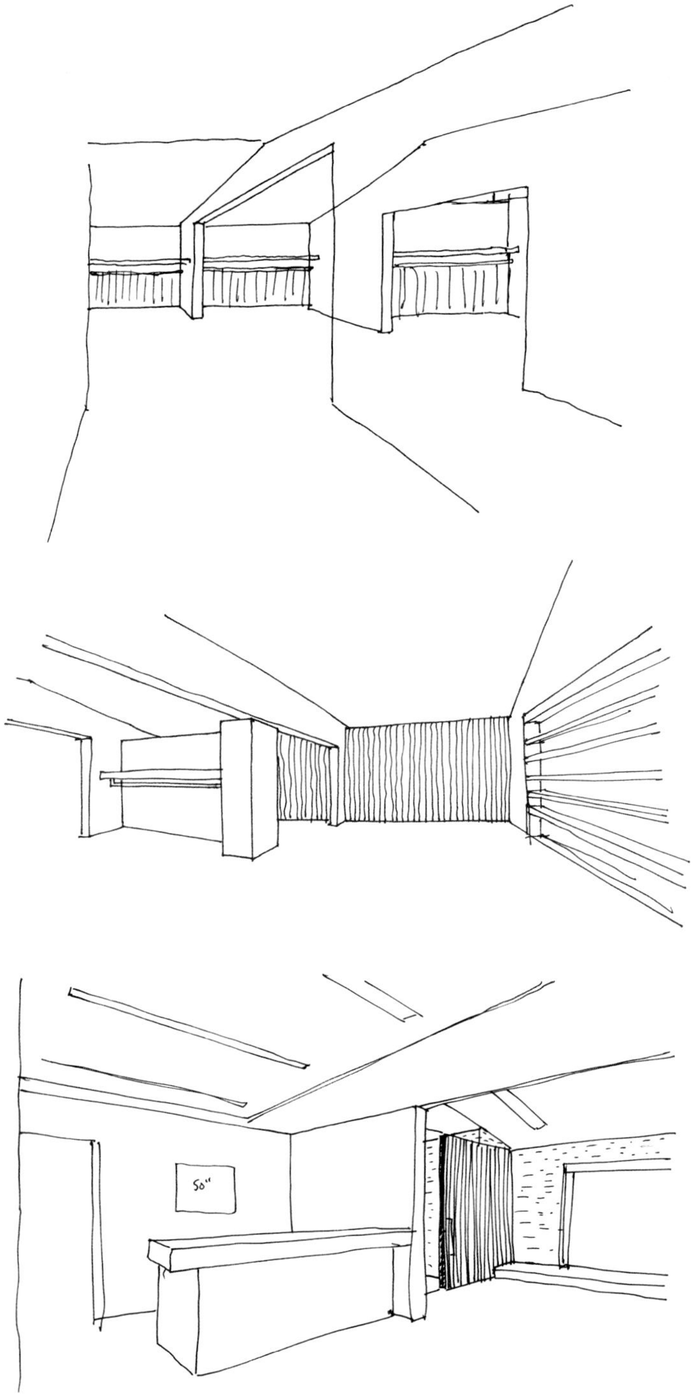

Entry door studies

Lounge

Sales area at storefront

Display desk

JENNI KAYNE STORE

Palo Alto, 2016

Jenni Kayne's Bay Area outpost reimagines the brand while retaining its established elements, such as integrally lit display shelves, bleached walnut and brass display cases, white brick walls and the use of daylight.

A custom-designed white brick facade references the storefronts of typical California freestanding retail locations. Tall wood-framed display windows and oversized bleached walnut entry doors welcome customers into the Stanford Shopping Mall store.

Warm, natural materials dominate the minimalist interior, while invisible light sources, a white wood ceiling and unfilled travertine floors frame the display cases.

The clean and straightforward lines of the display cases are designed for flexible multifunctionality, allowing them to showcase both home and fashion merchandise. Light and views are allowed in and strategically designed to highlight, reflect and complement the brand's natural, calm product line.

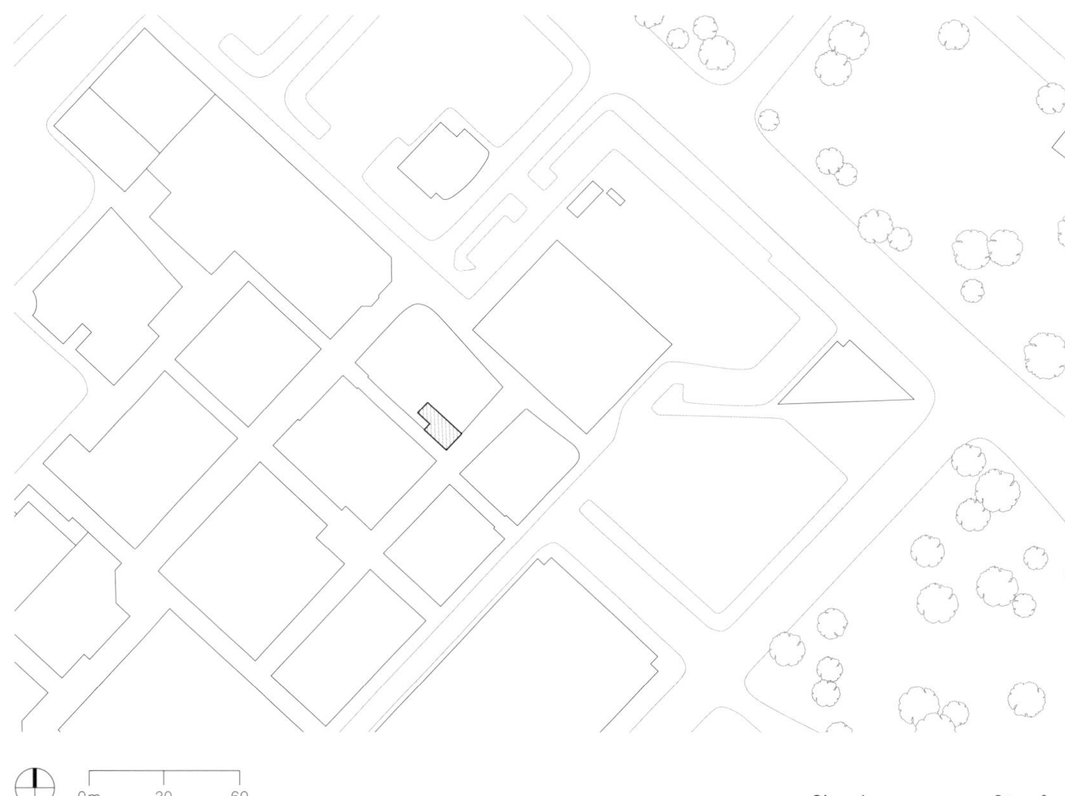

Site plan

Storefront

jenni kayne
jenni kayne
jenni kayne

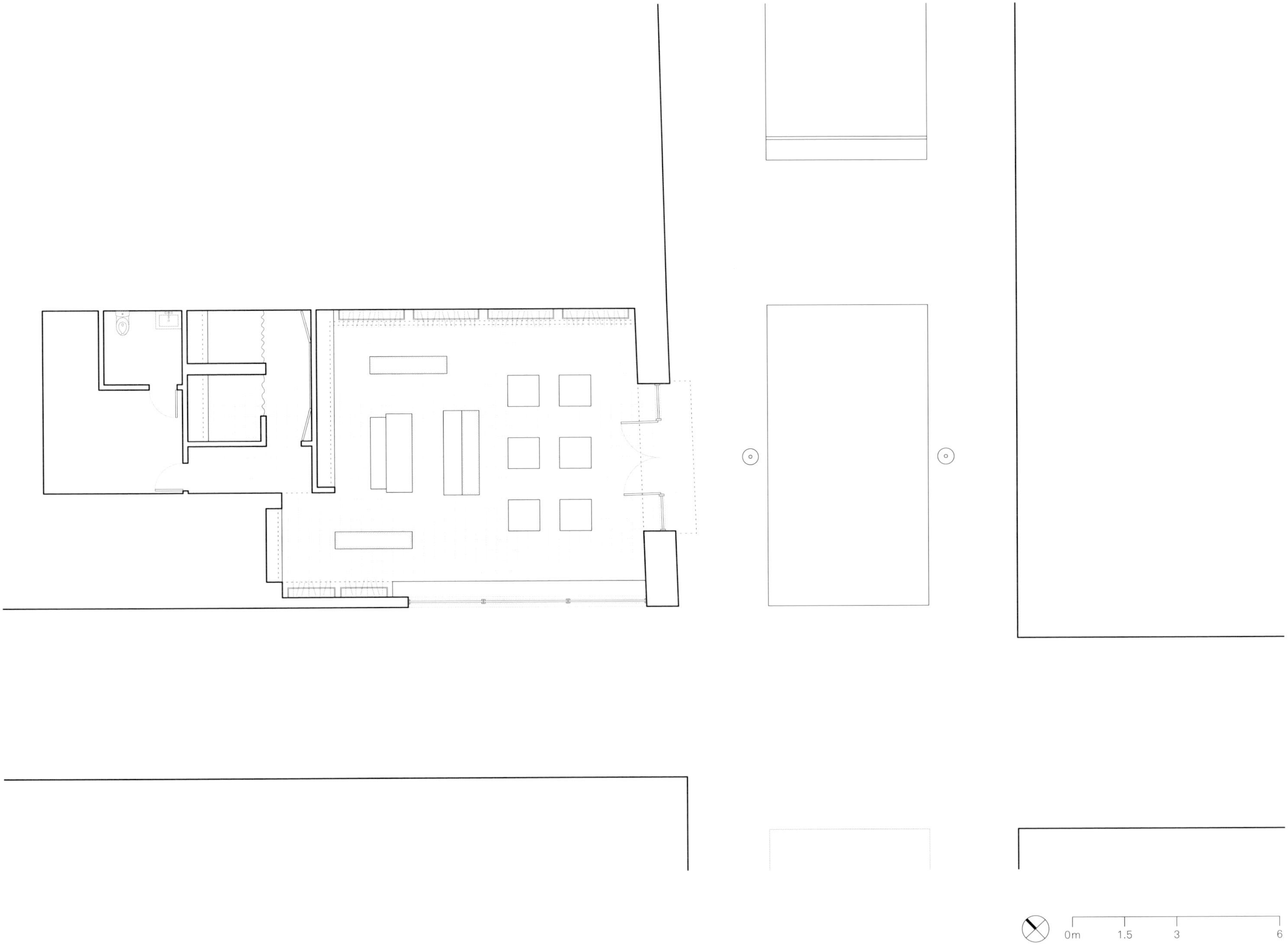

Floor plan

Main sales area

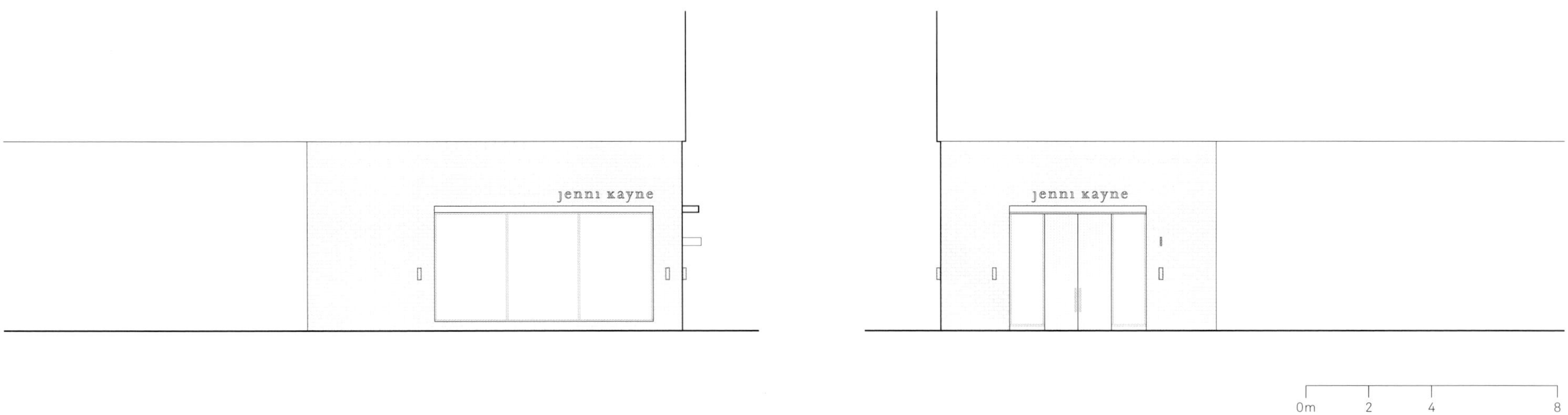

Exterior elevations

Entry door Hanging display Cash wrap Display shelves

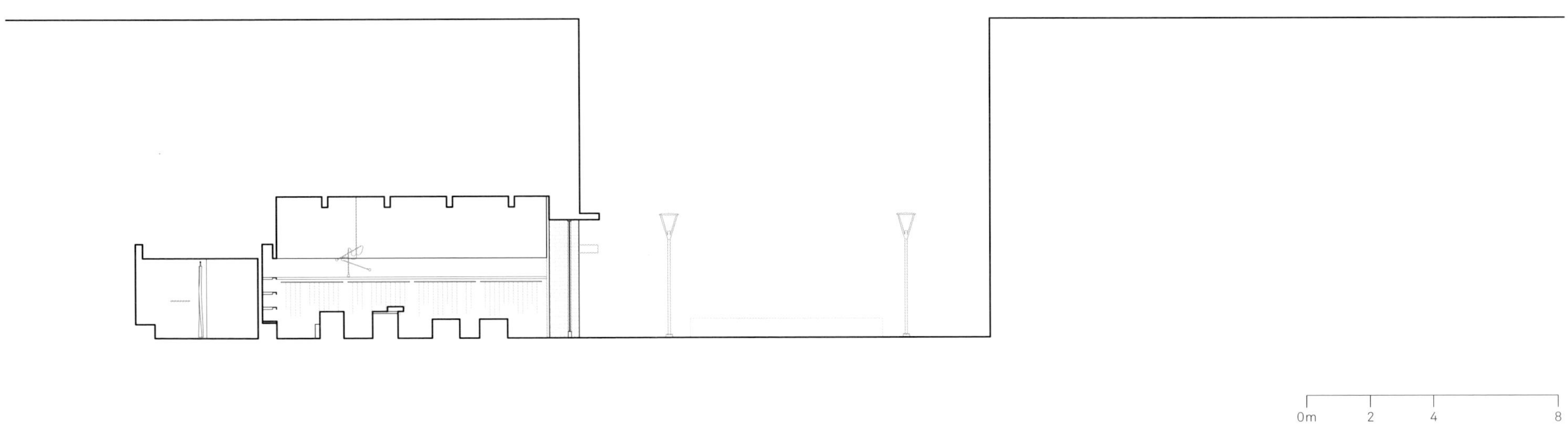

Section

Display shelves

HELMUT LANG STORE

Los Angeles, 2015

The new West Hollywood flagship store designed for fashion brand Helmut Lang, is located in an existing 3,000-square-foot, two-story building on Melrose Avenue. The design of the store connects the gallery-like, grayscale minimalism of the early stores to present day Los Angeles, integrating contemporary art, concealed lighting and contrasting raw and refined finishes.

The loft-like interior is clad in smooth, troweled and textured plaster walls and polished concrete floors, lined with display furniture made with stainless steel and charred wood. Natural and artificial lighting animate the space. New openings, cut through the walls and roof, bounce natural light deep into the interior, creating a luminous space. At the rear of the space, a large roof light was combined with a planting bed of the same shape on the floor, creating the effect of a courtyard to draw patrons into the space. Concealed LED lighting forms linear layers of light close to the clothing.

The store as art gallery concept is meant to recall the original Helmut Lang interiors, and to reimagine the concept for Los Angeles, incorporating natural light and planting. Los Angeles based artists were engaged to contribute to the design—a molded plaster screed by Mark Hagen was installed at the entry, creating a veil to the street, and RETNA custom painted the display tables. A vintage Cite daybed designed by Charlotte Perriand and Le Corbusier anchors the small room at the rear of the store.

Site plan

Entry ramp

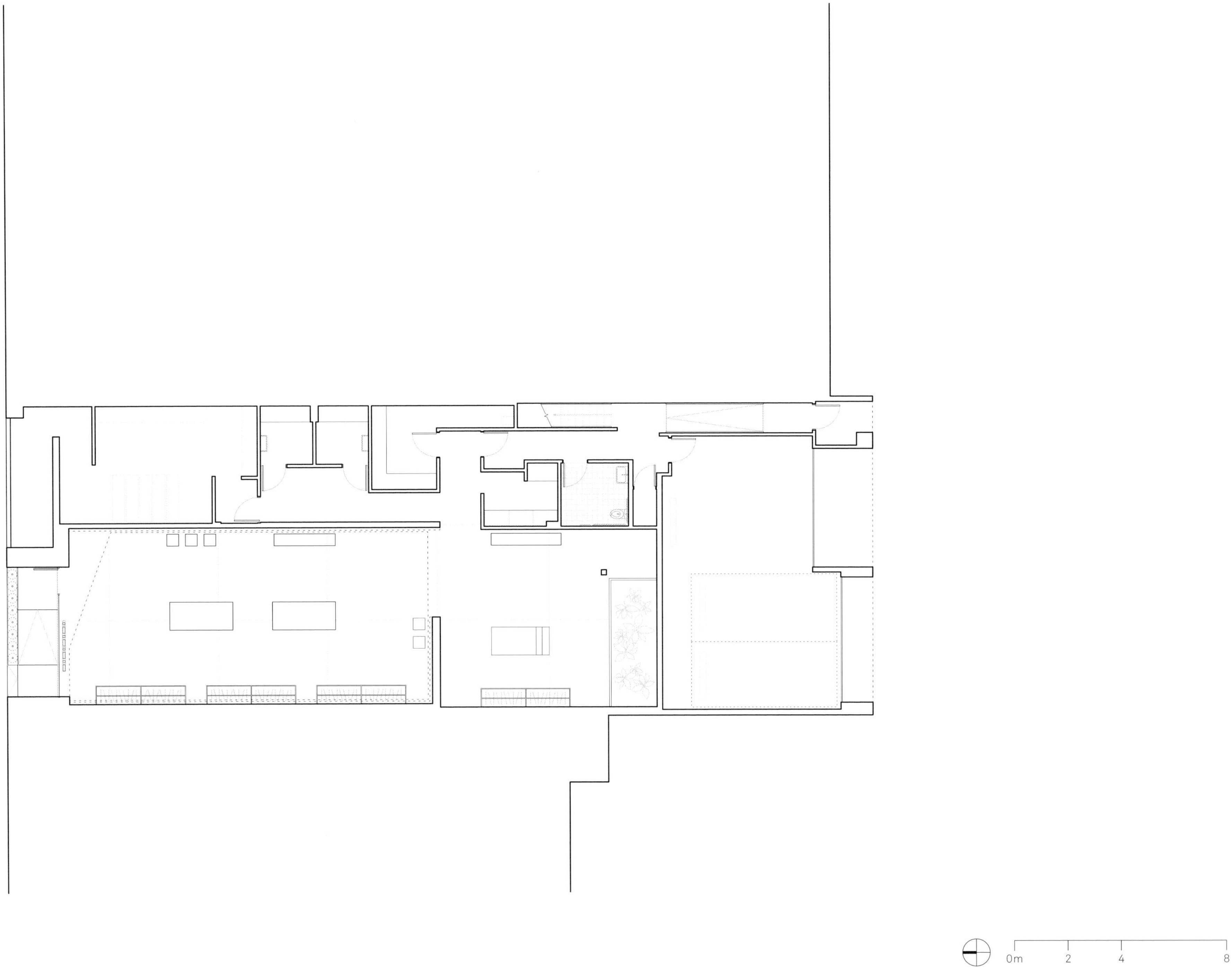

Floor plan

Two-story sales area

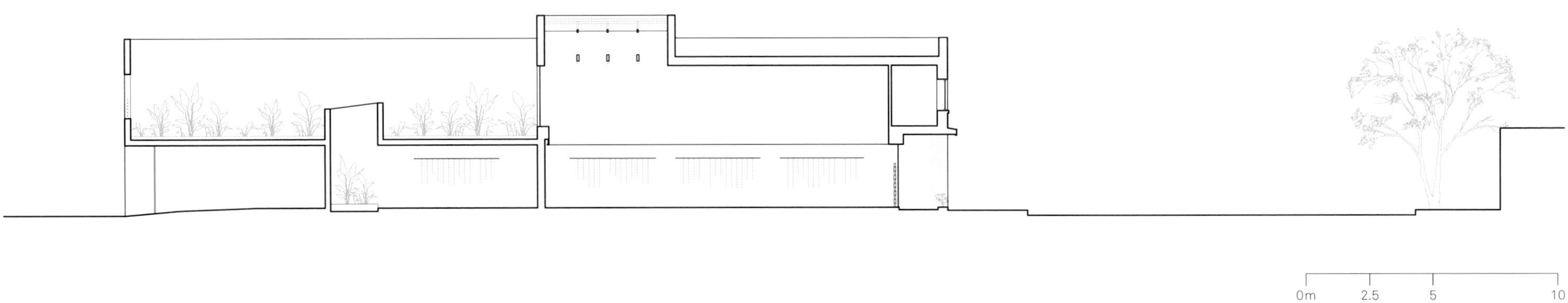

Longitudinal section

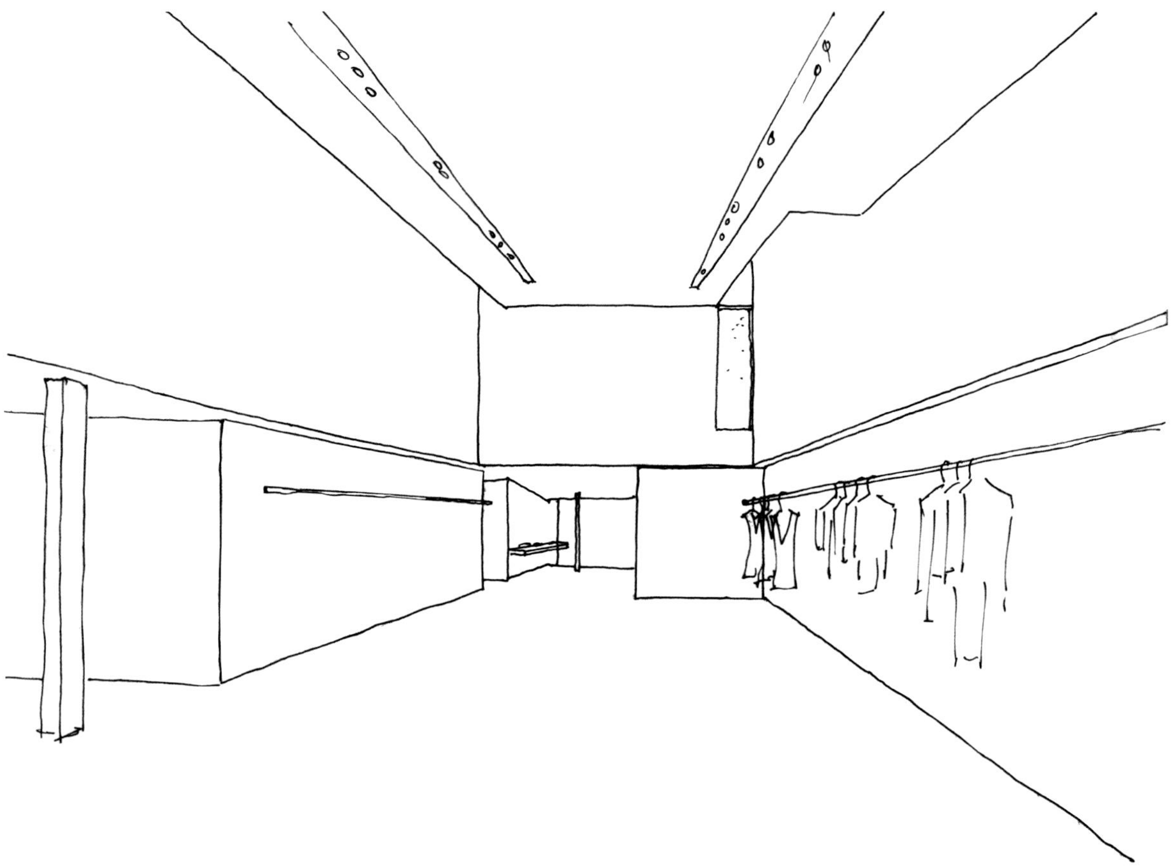

Perspective study

Two-story sales area

Sales area at courtyard

View to entry

View of both sales areas

COLLABORATORS

Ileana Acevedo, Alexander Babich, Stephen Baron, **Paulina Benavides**, Brandon Bown, Tracy Bremer, Jamie Bush, Alexis Carver, Christian Ceci, **Anthony Chieh**, **Tiara Chu**, Sunny Colvey, Greg Corso, Erin Cuevas, Lindsey Currey, Daniel Dunham, Jeff Dunn, Courtney Embrey, **Sarah Etaat**, **John Farrace**, **Lolade Frankel**, Tom Greek, Moira Henry, Wren Hoffman, Nicholas Hopson, Ashley James, **Sana Jihani**, **Andrew Kim**, Prajwal Krishna, Keith Krumwiede, Eunice Lee, Jared Levy, Kristina Loock, Jenny Ly, Christopher McMillan, Hiro Miura, Travis Muroki, **Mohamed Nazmy**, Makiko Nishida, Susan Nwankpa, Gregg Oelker, Monica Oller, Sylwia Pasciak, Meaghan Pohl, **Emmanuelle Raoul-Duval**, **Ryan Ripoli**, Klara Rodstrom, Jaime Roveri, Noah Rubin, **Alexander Sheft**, Kazushige Shichishima, Evan Shieh, Caroline Smogorzewski, Hana Shokr, **Jihun Son**, **Nazifa Virani**, Alex Whitehead, Phillip Williams, **Riko Yoshida**, Lillian Zeinalzadegan

Current Standard team
Past employees and collaborators

Jeffrey Allsbrook and Silvia Kuhle, both educated and apprenticed in Europe and the United States, are partners at Standard, a 20-person architecture and interior design practice.

CREDITS

BOOK CONCEPT
Standard

GRAPHIC DESIGN AND PRODUCTION TEAM
John Farrace and Hana Shokr, assisted by Nazifa Virani

DRAWINGS
Hana Shokr, assisted by Paulina Benavides, Tracy Bremer, Anthony Chieh, Tiara Chu, Lindsey Currey, Courtney Embrey, Sarah Etaat, John Farrace, Lolade Frankel, Sana Jihani, Andrew Kim, Mohamed Nazmy, Ryan Ripoli, Alexander Sheft, Kyle Reckling and Nazifa Virani

ESSAY
Mimi Zeiger

SKETCHES
Jeffrey Allsbrook

PHOTOGRAPHY
Jeffrey Allsbrook: pp. 69, 73 left, 75, 76–77, 83, 85, 87, 89, 113, 119

Kelly Barrie: pp. 57, 90, 91

Benny Chan, fotoworks: pp. 11, 13, 15, 17, 19, 21, 23, 24–25, 27, 29, 31, 33, 35, 36–37, 39, 41, 43, 45, 47, 49, 50, 51, 52, 53, 54–55, 59, 61, 63, 65, 66–67, 79, 81, 92, 93, 94–95, 97, 99, 101, 103, 105, 106, 107, 109, 111, 115, 117, 121, 123, 125, 127, 129, 131, 132, 133, 135, 137, 139, 141, 143, 145, 147, 149, 151, 153, 154, 155, 156–157

Lee Manning: p. 73 right

Robert Wedemeyer: p. 71

We thank Benny Chan for his generosity in contributing his photography of Standard's projects to this book.

The art shown in the Hillside Gallery photography is by Caio Fonseca, the art shown in the Kayne Griffin Corcoran Gallery photography is by Daniel Knorr and James Turrell, and the art shown in the Maccarone Gallery photography is by Carol Bove, Alex Hubbard, and Joe Zucker.

Artifice Press Limited
298 Regents Park Road, London, N3 2SZ
United Kingdom

+44 (0)20 8371 4000
office@artificeonline.com
www.artificeonline.com

Designed by Artifice Press.

British Library in Cataloguing Data
A CIP record for this book is available from the British Library.

ISBN 978-1-911339-04-5

Artifice Press is an environmentally responsible company. *Standard Architecture Design* is printed on sustainably sourced paper.

Printed by CPi Colour, London.

Artifice